Practice Using
MS-DOS® 6.2

Lynda Armbruster
Rancho Santiago College

COLLEGE

Practice Using MS-DOS 6.2

Library of Congress Catalog No.: 93-86967

Bundle ISBN: 1-56529-718-0

Practice Using Workbook ISBN: 1-56529-674-5

97   10   9   8   7

Interpretation of the printing code: the rightmost double-digit number is the year of the book's printing; the rightmost single-digit number, the number of the book's printing. For example, a printing code of 94-1 shows that the first printing of the book occurred in 1994.

Screens reproduced in this book were created using Collage Plus from Inner Media, Inc., Hollis, NH.

Practice Using MS-DOS 6.2 is based on MS-DOS 6.2.

Publisher: David P. Ewing

Director of Publishing: Michael Miller

Director of Operations & Editing: Chris Katsaropoulos

Book Designer: Amy Peppler-Adams

Production Team: Angela Bannan, Danielle Bird, Paula Carroll, Jenny Kucera, Joy Dean Lee, Beth Lewis, Nanci Sears Perry, Caroline Roop, Marc Shecter, Kris Simmons, Donna Winter, Robert Wolf, Lillian Yates

About the Author

Lynda Armbruster is a professor at Rancho Santiago College in Santa Ana, California, who began working with the DOS operating system shortly after its introduction in 1981. She has worked with computers for 30 years, including operating environments such as NetWare, UNIX, VM, CMS, VMS, and CP/M, and is a Certified NetWare Instructor and Certified NetWare Engineer. Lynda teaches courses in computer literacy, DOS, Lotus 1-2-3, NetWare system administration, and Internet basics, as well as graduate computer courses at Webster University in Irvine, California.

Prior to beginning her academic teaching career in 1986, Lynda was a computer industry trainer and technical writer. She received an MBA from National University and is working toward a PhD in Instructional Technology at the University of Southern California. Lynda and her husband Tom, a math teacher at San Marino High School, reside in Tustin with their three cats. Her adult son, Ed Kennedy, lives nearby in Irvine, California.

Editorial Director
Carol Crowell

Managing Editor
Sheila B. Cunningham

Senior Editor
Jeannine Freudenberger

Production Editor
Colleen Rainsberger

Editorial Coordinator
Elizabeth D. Brown

Composed in *Cheltenham* and *MCPdigital* by Que Corporation

Preface

Rationale for This Series

In response to requests from college instructors, Que College has designed the *Practice Using* series as a companion text to the *Using* series, Que's most successful line of books. Each *Using* book is both a tutorial and a reference for the beginning- to intermediate-level user. *Using* books help beginning students learn the software and its use, and provide many valuable tips and techniques for intermediate users. Que's *Using* books are recognized for presenting highly technical information in an understandable form. By bringing the *Using* books into the classroom with *Practice Using*, Que College offers the source to which professionals have turned at work for years, along with the support that instructors and students need.

Organization of the *Using* Books

Using books are designed to "grow" with readers, providing the tutorial and reference material that readers need as they move from learning the basics to investigating ways to become more productive with advanced features of the software. Each book teaches the reader how the software works, how to use the most common procedures and commands, and, finally, how to take advantage of more advanced procedures and concepts.

Each chapter is a task-oriented module that covers a group of related features. The chapters contain the following basic elements:

- The chapter introduction discusses the primary tasks covered in the chapter.

- Text and graphics explain the program's operation and features; for example, menu options, function keys, and special indicators on-screen.

- Conceptual text and graphics illustrate more difficult concepts.

- Numbered steps with supporting screen illustrations present procedures. The illustrations confirm that the user has successfully completed part of a procedure. Supporting examples illustrate the potential of the software, the common uses of a particular feature, and effective usage of that feature.

- Tips, cautions, and notes throughout chapters present techniques, dangers, and helpful information relating to specific procedures explained at that point in the text.

- Chapter summaries briefly review the features and procedures presented in the chapter and conclude with a sentence or two describing the main focus of the next chapter.

Organization of the *Practice Using* Books

The accompanying *Practice Using* book applies the information presented in the *Using* book so that students can practice new skills and reinforce concepts as they progress. Students will refer to the *Using* book to answer the questions, work the directed exercises, and solve the problems in *Practice Using*. As a result of this approach, students learn both the substance of the software and, importantly, research techniques for finding answers to questions.

The *Practice Using* series has these key features:

- Matching questions for key terms

- Multiple-choice and true/false questions

- Directed, step-by-step exercises for practicing skills described in the corresponding *Using* chapter

- Continuing problems built around case studies as the book progresses

- Challenge problems for more advanced students or for completion as part of a team effort

Projects and exercises are weighted according to what instructors emphasize in the classroom. As a result, more attention is given to the most frequently used features.

Titles

The *Practice Using* series includes the following books at the time this book was published.

Practice Using MS-DOS 5	1-56529-434-3
Practice Using Excel 4 for Windows	1-56529-413-9
Practice Using Lotus 1-2-3 Release 2.2	1-56529-719-9
Practice Using Lotus 1-2-3 Release 2.3	1-56529-717-2
Practice Using Lotus 1-2-3 Release 2.4	1-56529-436-X
Practice Using Novell NetWare	1-56529-433-5
Practice Using Windows 3.1	1-56529-432-7
Practice Using WordPerfect 5.1	1-56529-437-8
Practice Using WordPerfect 6	1-56529-596-X

Supplements

Que College has developed an *Instructor's Manual* and an *Instructor's Resource Disk*, both available at no additional charge upon adoption of the text. The *Instructor's Manual* includes a suggested course outline, teaching tips, answers to all the questions in *Practice Using*, and additional test questions. The *Instructor's Resource Disk* includes the entire *Instructor's Manual* in ASCII format so that you can copy the files into your word processor, modify existing material, add your own notes or questions, and make printouts for students as desired. In addition, the *Instructor's Resource Disk* contains separate data files for the exercises and projects in the *Practice Using* text. Upon adoption, you may copy these files onto disks or onto your network for students.

For more information call

1-800-428-5331

Acknowledgments

I have had a lot of assistance and encouragement from many people as this project developed. I want to express my sincere thanks to everyone who helped, and especially to the following people:

My loving husband, Tom, for all his support and understanding while this book was being written, and for constantly bringing me flowers ever since we met.

My son, Ed, for building the bookshelves to hold all my reference materials. Thanks for your efforts.

My best friends Myrna Bravo and Joy Colby, for encouraging me and being like sisters. I can't remember how I got through life before knowing you.

My mother-in-law Eva Armbruster, for being the best family anyone could ask for.

Also thanks to my boss, John Howe, and others at Rancho Santiago College for encouragement and inspiration, especially Carolyn Breeden, Avril Lovell, and Ethel Kilkeary.

Jane Rosenkranz, Joyce Gaspard, Herb Cohen, Dave Moore, Doug Robinson, and the rest of my colleagues at Webster University for being so terrific to work with over the years.

The thousands of students who have attended my computer classes over the years. Thanks for teaching me so much.

Meta Hirschl, Carol Crowell, Betsy Brown, Colleen Rainsberger, Christina Martin, and the rest of the hard-working Que College team who made this book possible.

Cindy Hollingsworth of Indiana University-Purdue University at Indianapolis for an excellent technical review of the manuscript and suggestions that made this a better book.

And last but not least, thanks to BB, Pixel, and Miss Kitty-Kitty for providing daily cuddling and entertainment.

Que College is grateful for the assistance provided by the following reviewers: Cletus Stripling, University of Georgia; Norm Sondak, San Diego State; and Allan Rowland, Ivy Tech.

Trademark Acknowledgments

Conventions Used in This Book

Certain conventions are followed in this book and in the accompanying *Using* book to help you understand the questions and problems. The conventions are explained more fully in the *Using* book.

Names of files, directories, and DOS commands are written in all capital letters. Names of keys appear as they appear on a standard keyboard. Keys pressed in combination are joined by a hyphen (Ctrl-H).

Words and phrases you are to type and keys you are to press appear in **boldfaced type**. Screen messages and quotations from the computer screen appear in a `special typeface`.

Table of Contents

5 Understanding Files and Directories 51

16   Understanding Batch Files   191

DOS and the Personal Computer

Chapter Summary

Chapter 1 is the first of four chapters devoted to explaining the fundamental role of DOS in a working PC. Since the release of the IBM PC, more than 95 percent of all the tens of millions of personal computers sold have used MS-DOS as the operating system. The objective of this chapter is to familiarize less experienced computer users with the inner workings of computer systems.

Chapter 1 examines today's PCs, exploring the major components of the PC and addressing the use of system and peripheral hardware. It gives you a feel not only for your system but also for systems with different keyboards, displays, and peripherals. It explains the role of DOS in relation to the system and covers the following main points:

- MS-DOS stands for Microsoft Disk Operating System.

- MS-DOS provides the software support necessary to make your computer operate efficiently. It also enables you to run other software applications.

- The *central processing unit* (CPU) is the brain of the computer system. All other devices attached to the system are peripherals and are controlled by DOS and the CPU.

- Most DOS software operates within the 640K barrier. Unused addresses from 640K to 1M are known as *upper memory blocks* and can be used to run programs and device drivers. Major portions of DOS can be loaded into the upper memory area.

- The *LIM 3.2* and *LIM 4.0 Expanded Memory Specifications* (EMS and EEMS) can use conventional memory addresses (those below 1M) to act as a window into added memory of up to 16M.

- The *Extended Memory Specification* (XMS) is a linear extension of memory addresses above the 1M mark. Few DOS programs currently can use extended memory, but Windows and Windows programs routinely load into extended memory addresses.

- Floppy disks and hard disks use a magnetic technology similar to cassette recorders and VCRs to store data permanently as named files. CD-ROMs and optical drives someday will be the dominant method for storing files.

Chapter Outline

I. PC Hardware

    A. The PC Architecture
    B. Computer Memory
    C. Peripheral Devices

II. What Happens When the Power Is Turned On?

III. DOS and Random-Access Memory

    A. Conventional Memory
    B. Expanded Memory
    C. Extended Memory

IV. DOS and Disks

Active Learning

Key Term Matching

Match the following key terms with the definitions listed after them.

_e_ 1. Peripheral

_m_ 2. Floppy disk

_j_ 3. RAM

_c_ 4. COMMAND.COM

_x_ 5. CD-ROM

___ 6. Protected mode

_j_ 7. CPU

_p_ 8. Expanded memory

___ 9. ROM

_a_ 10. Booting

_i_ 11. Hard disk

_d_ 12. POST

_q_ 13. Conventional memory

_o_ 14. Binary

_k_ 15. Extended memory

_s_ 16. Real mode

_b_ 17. ASCII

_h_ 18. Motherboard

_n_ 19. CMOS

_k_ 20. File

Definitions

a. The process of starting the computer by turning on the power.

b. The code used with PCs to represent letters, numerals, graphics characters, and common commands used by the CPU.

c. Refers to a mode of operation that lets the CPU address memory above 1M with the capability to run more than one program at the same time with each program protected from the actions of the other programs.

d. The self test the computer runs when the power is first turned on.

e. Any device connected to your computer's CPU, either with an expansion slot card or plugged into a port.

f. A non-volatile form of memory that permanently stores instructions for the computer.

g. Memory that is restricted to one megabyte.

h. The main circuit board of your system which contains the core group of components needed to build a complete computer system.

i. A non-removable, high-capacity, rigid set of platters sealed inside a dust-free casing used for storing files.

j. A volatile form of memory that acts somewhat like an electronic chalkboard where information can be written and erased.

k. A memory specification that allows memory addresses above one megabyte to become available to your programs.

l. The microprocessor chip capable of receiving input, processing data, and producing the results as output.

m. A wafer-thin plastic disk coated with a magnetic emulsion and encased within a protective sleeve.

n. A special kind of chip that stores information about the system's configuration, such as the system's date and time settings; these chips are used because they need only a small amount of power that can be supplied by a battery.

o. A numbering system made up of digits 0 and 1 and used by computers because it can easily be expressed with electrical circuits.

p. Up to 16 megabytes of memory on a special memory board that can be used to store information that is swapped from the memory board to a page frame in system memory and back again as needed.

q. An optical disk, which is a hard plastic disk containing an embedded sheet of metal foil covered with pits or indentations that can be read by a laser.

r. A collection of information stored by DOS.

s. The limited capabilities to run software applications of the 8088 and 8086 processors.

t. Provides the user interface to DOS and its job is to evaluate whether commands presented to DOS from the keyboard or from batch files are legal.

Multiple-Choice Questions

_____ 1. The heart and soul of any personal computer is its

      a. modem capabilities.
      b. central processing unit.
      c. expansion slots.
      d. peripherals.
      e. parallel and serial communications ports.

_____ 2. The volatile form of memory that holds information only when electrically powered is called

      a. DOS.
      b. ASCII.
      c. ROM.
      d. RAM.
      e. CPU.

_____ 3. When you boot your computer, the first thing it does is known as the

      a. POST.
      b. CMOS.
      c. RAM.
      d. CPM.
      e. ASCII.

_____ 4. The name of the file that provides the user interface to DOS is:

      a. CONFIG.SYS
      b. AUTOEXEC.BAT
      c. MSDOS.SYS
      d. IO.SYS
      e. COMMAND.COM

_____ 5. A hard plastic disk that is optically read by a laser is known as a

      a. floppy disk.
      b. CD-ROM.
      c. hard disk.
      d. magnetic disk.
      e. protected mode.

True/False Questions

1. The LIM 3.2 and LIM 4.0 Extended Memory Specifications (XMS) can use conventional memory addresses to act as a window into added memory of up to 16 megabytes.

2. Most DOS software operates within the 640K barrier.

3. The Expanded Memory Specification (EMS) is a linear extension of memory addresses above the 1M mark.

4. Most optical disks available today are of the WORM variety.

5. Floppy disks and hard disks use a magnetic technology similar to cassette recorders and VCRs to store data permanently as named files.

▶ Directed Exercises

Exercise 1: Locating Components

This exercise is designed to help you become familiar with the various components of your computer.

The Computer Display (Monitor)

1. Locate the On/Off switch or button. If you have a switch, it may be labeled with a ø to indicate Off and 1 to indicate On. Don't worry if your switch is not labeled.

2. Locate the brightness and contrast controls.

3. Locate the power cable and the monitor cable that plug into the back of the computer.

4. Determine which type of display you have (such as EGA, VGA, SVGA, or LCD).

The System Box (Computer)

1. Locate the On/Off switch. Note that 0 indicates Off and 1 indicates On.

2. Locate the floppy drive(s) on the front of the system box. If you have two floppy drives, locate Drive A:, then locate Drive B:. What are the size and disk capacity of each drive?

3. Locate the power cord. This cord is usually connected in the back at the power supply.

The Printer

1. Locate the On/Off switch.

2. What type is this printer (laser, inkjet, or dot-matrix)?

3. Is this printer connected to a serial or parallel port on the system box?

Exercise 2: Looking at DOS, Hardware, and Applications Relationships

DOS is the manager for technical details of a computer as well as a means of file storage. Draw a diagram that depicts the relationship among DOS, hardware, and application programs.

Exercise 3: Reading about Microprocessors

Using MS-DOS 6.2, Special Edition, mentions the Intel 80286, 80386, and 80486 microprocessors. Research this topic and write a one-page report describing the fundamental differences between these three members of the Intel family and compare them to the newest member, the *Pentium* microprocessor. Be sure to include your opinion on which processor you think would be most appropriate for your personal use today.

Answers to Odd-Numbered Questions

Key Term Matching Questions

1. e		11. i	
3. j		13. g	
5. q		15. k	
7. e		17. b	
9. f		19. n	

Multiple-Choice Questions

1. b
3. a
5. b

True/False Questions

1. F
3. F
5. T

Starting DOS

Chapter Summary

Chapter 2 provides an overview of the process of booting a PC and explains important concepts, including how to control the booting process by setting up multiple configurations. It also explains how to load device drivers and control the environment of your PC, covering the following key points:

- To boot a computer, you can use only disks (floppy or hard) that you have formatted with the /S switch of the FORMAT command or that you have made bootable by using the SYS command.

- Booting from a hard disk is usually more efficient than booting from a floppy disk, but sometimes you need a bootable floppy disk.

- The CONFIG.SYS file configures your computer's DOS session.

- You can create menus by adding to CONFIG.SYS and AUTOEXEC.BAT sections that allow for multiple configurations.

- AUTOEXEC.BAT is a normal batch file that is run each time the computer boots. This file further refines the computer's configuration by running commands that need to be entered only once.

Chapter Outline

I. Booting Your Computer

    A. Understanding the Boot Disk
    B. Booting from a Floppy or a Hard Disk

II. System Configuration

    A. CONFIG.SYS
    B. AUTOEXEC.BAT

III. Controlling the Boot Process

IV. Creating Multiple Configurations

    A. Creating a Default Configuration
    B. Displaying Color Menus
    C. Using the Configuration Menu as a System Menu

Active Learning

Key Term Matching

Match the following key terms with the definitions listed after them.

1. AUTOEXEC.BAT		11. BUFFERS
2. FORMAT /S		12. HIGHMEM.SYS
3. ECHO OFF		13. DEVICEHIGH
4. LASTDRIVE		14. IO.SYS
5. MSDOS.SYS		15. STACKS
6. Cold boot		16. DEVICE
7. F8		17. FORMAT /B
8. :END		18. Warm boot
9. CONFIG.SYS		19. COMMAND.COM
10. Ctrl-F8		20. Ctrl-F5

Definitions

a. Copies two hidden boot files to a newly prepared disk but leaves off the operating system and bootstrap loader.

b. This file must be the first physical file on a bootable disk and the first directory entry in the root directory of the disk.

c. If you press this key combination, the boot process skips CONFIG.SYS and AUTOEXEC.BAT and doesn't load DoubleSpace.

d. If present, this file is automatically loaded during the boot process and consists of DOS commands.

e. Sets the number of file buffers DOS uses in transferring data to and from disk.

f. Causes MS-DOS to prompt you to confirm each CONFIG.SYS command.

g. The main program that gets loaded when the computer is booted.

h. Occurs when you turn on the power switch to your system, triggering the POST to check the condition of the system's major components and of RAM.

i. CONFIG.SYS command that specifies the highest valid disk drive letter.

j. Pressing this key combination allows you to process CONFIG.SYS and AUTOEXEC.BAT interactively without loading DoubleSpace.

k. Prepares a floppy disk with all files to make it bootable.

l. Loads a device driver in conventional memory.

m. This file must be the second entry in the root directory of a bootable disk.

n. Marks a section in a batch file that lets DOS skip over the sections that haven't been chosen and lets any commands added by software installation take effect.

o. The Extended Memory Manager that allows access to memory addresses above one megabyte.

p. CONFIG.SYS command that sets the number and size of stacks used to process hardware interrupts.

q. When used in a batch file, suppresses the display of the commands as they are processed.

r. Triggered when you press the Ctrl-Alt-Del keys all at the same time; bypasses the preliminary self-test and moves directly to the loading of DOS.

s. Loads a device driver into upper memory.

t. Each line in this file contains a DOS command that tells DOS to enhance the DOS configuration.

Multiple-Choice Questions

____ 1. The process of restarting the computer by pressing the Ctrl-Alt-Del keys all at the same time is called a

    a. cold boot.
    b. DOS prompt.
    c. warm boot.
    d. syntax.
    e. POST.

____ 2. The process of restarting a PC by turning off the power switch is called a

    a. cold boot.
    b. DOS prompt.
    c. warm boot.
    d. syntax.
    e. POST.

____ 3. If you use the FORMAT /B command on a disk, you can later use the ____ command to finish the job of making the disk bootable.

    a. IO.SYS
    b. COMMAND.COM
    c. FORMAT /S
    d. SYS
    e. MSDOS.SYS

_____ 4. During the boot process, the boot program looks for the _____ file in the root directory to install any device drivers or special configuration information.

    a. POST
    b. ROM BIOS
    c. AUTOEXEC.BAT
    d. COMMAND.COM
    e. CONFIG.SYS

2

_____ 5. If you press the _____ key(s) when the Starting MS-DOS... message appears, MS-DOS prompts you to confirm each CONFIG.SYS command.

    a. Ctrl-Alt-Del
    b. F8
    c. Ctrl-F5
    d. F5
    e. Ctrl-F8

True/False Questions

_____ 1. The default size of the DOS environment is only 9,256 bytes in length.

_____ 2. For a disk to be bootable, IO.SYS must be the first physical file on the disk.

_____ 3. The BUFFERS command can be put into the AUTOEXEC.BAT file to set the number of file buffers DOS uses in transferring data to and from disk.

_____ 4. When you warm boot the PC, the computer skips the preliminary POST operation.

_____ 5. If you press the F5 key when the Starting MS-DOS... message appears on-screen during the boot process, the boot process bypasses loading and processing both CONFIG.SYS and AUTOEXEC.BAT.

Directed Exercises

Exercise 1: Booting Your System with a "Cold Boot" and a "Warm Boot"

If your computer is on, turn it off. Wait at least ten seconds. Make sure that your monitor is on, and turn your computer back on. Watch for the following to take place:

- The system performing a memory (RAM) or POST check.

- A beep and activity starting on Drive A: and Drive B: (if installed).

- Activity on the hard disk, after the system checks any floppy drives that are installed.

- DOS being loaded into memory. You may notice some activity on Drive A: if you are using a boot disk, or on Drive C: (your hard disk).

- The CONFIG.SYS file being executed and the AUTOEXEC.BAT file being executed. (*Note:* This activity may not be apparent on-screen; see whether you can detect anything happening, but don't be dismayed if there are no messages or obvious signs.)

Follow these steps:

1. Write a one-sentence explanation of how and why you would perform a warm boot.

2. Take the steps to perform a warm boot and observe the similarities and differences between this type of boot and the previous one.

Exercise 2: Creating a CONFIG.SYS File

This exercise gives you practice creating a CONFIG.SYS file for your system. Write the commands on paper, but *do not enter the commands into the computer* at this time.

1. Write on paper what would be on the first line of the CONFIG.SYS file if you use the DEVICE command to load HIMEM.SYS.

2. What would the second line say to use the DOS command to specify that upper memory be used?

BUFFERS = 40, V

3. Write down what the third line would say to establish that 40 buffers can be used to transfer files.

FILES

4. What command would specify on the fourth line that DOS will make 60 file handles available so that 60 files can be open at one time?

LAST DRIVE

5. The fifth line should establish that Drive Z: is the highest drive present in the system, including drives created by DoubleSpace and all drives used by any network to which you might be connected.

STACKS

6. The sixth written command should specify that nine stacks of 256 bytes each are used to handle hardware interrupts.

7. After you have decided which commands to use and have written them on paper, verify with your instructor that they are correct.

Exercise 3: Creating an **AUTOEXEC.BAT** File

This exercise gives you practice creating an AUTOEXEC.BAT file for your system. Write the commands on paper but *do not enter the commands into the computer* at this time.

1. Write what the first line of the AUTOEXEC.BAT file would read if you were going to use the ECHO OFF command to suppress the display of the commands as they are processed.

IS

2. On the second line, write the command that clears the screen.

prompt pg

PATH C

3. Write the command on the third line that uses the PROMPT PG command to cause the DOS prompt to show the currently logged drive and path.

4. On the fourth line, write the command to use the PATH command to specify that DOS can search the C:\DOS, C:\WINDOWS, C:\, and C:\MOUSE.

SET Temp
= C:\TEMP

5. The fifth line's command should use the SET command to establish the TEMP as C:\TEMP.

6. The final line executes the MOUSE program.

7. After you have decided which commands to use and written them on paper, verify with your instructor that they are correct.

Answers to Odd-Numbered Questions

Key Term Matching Questions

1. d	11. e
3. q	13. s
5. m	15. p
7. f	17. a
9. t	19. g

Multiple-Choice Questions

1. c
3. d
5. b

True/False Questions

1. F
3. F
5. T

Using DOS Commands

Chapter Summary

Chapter 3 introduces DOS commands and explains how to use them. It introduces you to the concepts behind issuing commands at the command line and explains syntax, parameters, and switches. It covers important keys, as well as information on how to access the DOS built-in help system.

Even though each DOS command has its own characteristics, it also has a defined syntax that may or may not include parameters and switches. The basic knowledge of how to issue DOS commands is an important ingredient in your mastery of DOS. Chapter 3 covers the following major concepts:

- Commands that you enter at the DOS prompt are your way of requesting and receiving operating system services.

- The proper phrasing of each DOS command is called the command's *syntax*.

- In addition to the name of the command, a syntax line can contain parameters and switches.

- You can use the /? command-line switch or the HELP command to get help on any DOS command.

- You can edit a DOS command line by using special DOS editing keys.

- Commands that take file name specifications as parameters accept wildcard characters (? and *) as substitutes for position-matching in file name parameters.

Chapter Outline

I. Understanding DOS Commands

    A. Internal versus External
    B. Making Sure DOS Can Find External Commands

II. Understanding the Elements of a DOS Command

    A. The Command Syntax
    B. The Command-Line Parameters
    C. The Optional Switches

III. Getting Help

    A. Using the Command-Line Help Switch
    B. Using the On-Line Help System

IV. Issuing DOS Commands

    A. Editing and Canceling Commands
    B. Using Scroll Control
    C. Using Wildcards in DOS Commands

Active Learning

Key Term Matching

Match the following key terms with the definitions listed after them.

_____ 1. F3
_____ 2. *.*
_____ 3. Ctrl-S
_____ 4. Parameters
_____ 5. DIR /?
_____ 6. Internal commands
_____ 7. Ctrl-Home
_____ 8. Syntax
_____ 9. Alt-C
_____ 10. External commands

_____ 11. DIR /P
_____ 12. Backslash (\)
_____ 13. Keyword
_____ 14. Enter
_____ 15. Alt-N
_____ 16. Slash (/)
_____ 17. DIR /W
_____ 18. F1
_____ 19. Escape
_____ 20. Switch

3

Definitions

a. Pressing this key completes a command and stores it in the last command buffer.

b. The specific set of rules, similar to rules of grammar, that DOS requires when you issue commands; it describes the order in which you type the elements of the command.

c. Using this key copies all remaining characters from the preceding command line.

d. Used as separators or delimiters when specifying directory and file information.

e. Displays a list of files and subdirectories in a directory with pauses after each screenful of information.

f. This keystroke combination temporarily stops a scrolling screen until you press any key to restart the scrolling.

g. DOS commands that are stored as utility programs in a directory on your hard disk.

× , *⋆* h. The wildcard combination that represents all file names with any extension in a given subdirectory.

Escape i. This key cancels the current line and does not change the last command buffer.

Keyword j. All DOS commands begin with one of these; it identifies the action you want performed.

DIR /? k. Typing this command gives you a short summary help screen for the command used to display a list of files and subdirectories in a directory.

Alt-N l. When you use the on-line help system, using this key combination moves you to the next topic.

Switches m. A special kind of parameter that turns on an optional function of a command.

DIR/W n. Displays a list of files and subdirectories in a directory using the wide list format.

o. Commands that are provided by COMMAND.COM.

F1 p. Pressing this key while you are using the on-line help system displays context-sensitive help on using the on-line help system.

Fwd slash (/) q. A character that is used as a signal to DOS that the next character is a command-line switch.

r. When you use the on-line help system, this key displays the list of topics covered in the help system.

Parameter s. These are part of a command's syntax which refine the way a command is executed.

Ctrl-Home t. When you use the on-line help system, pressing this key combination moves you to the beginning of the current topic.

Multiple-Choice Questions

_____ 1. All DOS commands begin with a _____ that identifies the action you want performed.

    a. syntax
    b. parameter
    c. switch
    d. verb
    e. keyword

_____ 2. A storage area for command-line keystrokes is called an input

    a. delimiter.
    b. prompt.
    c. syntax.
    d. buffer.
    e. keystroke.

_____ 3. The _____ key cancels the current line and does not change the buffer.

    a. F3
    b. Enter
    c. Esc
    d. F6
    e. Ins

_____ 4. The specific order in which you type the elements of a DOS command is called the

    a. parameter.
    b. syntax.
    c. command.
    d. prompt.
    e. delimiter.

_____ 5. Commands that are built into the command processor and are immediately available at the command line are called

    a. DOS delimiters.
    b. external commands.
    c. DOS prompts.
    d. internal commands.
    e. DOS syntax.

3

_____ 6. An addition to a command that changes the way a command is executed is called

      a. syntax.
      b. delimiters.
      c. parameters.
      d. prompts.
      e. internal commands.

_____ 7. The _____ wildcard represents any single character when used in conjunction with a DOS command such as DIR.

      a. *
      b. \
      c. /
      d. ^
      e. ?

_____ 8. When using a switch or parameter with a DOS command, it must be preceded by the _____ character

      a. *
      b. \
      c. /
      d. ^
      e. ?

_____ 9. In order to execute a command, you type the name of the command and then press the _____ key.

      a. Enter
      b. Esc
      c. F3
      d. F1
      e. Ins

_____10. The command to display the directory listing one screen at a time is:

      a. DIR /w
      b. DIR /p
      c. DIR /c
      d. DIR /s
      e. DIR

True/False Questions

____ 1. As long as the DOS external commands are placed on a floppy disk, you can use it to boot the system.

____ 2. All DOS commands begin with a keyword that identifies the action you want performed.

____ 3. A switch is a special parameter that turns on an optional function of a command.

____ 4. You use the Escape key to select a menu command.

____ 5. DOS is not particular about which characters you use in a file name or an extension and will accept just about anything on the keyboard as a valid entry.

____ 6. There are several ways to access the DOS on-line help facility.

____ 7. A parameter can consist of up to three letters and represents the parts of a command line that provide DOS with the objects of the command's action.

____ 8. When you press F3 at the command line, DOS automatically enters all remaining characters from the preceding command line.

____ 9. When you use the on-line help system, pressing F1 displays context-sensitive help about the help system.

____ 10. In DOS commands such as DIR, the ? character represents any single character.

▶ # Directed Exercises

Exercise 1: Using the DIR Command with Wildcards

In this exercise, you practice using different variations of the DIR command. The exercise assumes that you are using a computer with a hard disk designated as Drive C:, and that there is a subdirectory named \DOS on that drive. Follow these steps:

1. At the DOS prompt, type **c:** and press **Enter**, and then type **cd**
   and press **Enter** again. Next, type **dir \dos** and press **Enter**.
   This enables you to view the entire contents of the subdirectory containing all the DOS files.

2. At the next DOS prompt, type **cd \dos** and press **Enter** again.
   This makes the DOS files subdirectory the default directory.

3. To see all files that end with the file extension EXE, type
   dir *.exe and press **Enter**.

   a. How many files are listed?

   b. What do all the files listed have in common?

   c. How much disk space is being occupied by the listed
      files?

4. Type **dir s?????.exe** and press **Enter**.

   a. How many files are listed?

   b. What are the differences in the file names?

5. Type **dir s*.??e** and press **Enter**.

   a. How did the results of this command compare to the step
      above?

   b. Were the results the same or different?

   c. After the command line, what does the first line displayed
      on-screen say?

6. To get information on a single file, enter the DIR command
   and follow it with the name of the file. Practice by typing
   dir chkdsk.exe and pressing **Enter**.

7. At the DOS prompt, type **dir > prn**, and press **Enter**. This command redirects the output normally sent to the screen to the
   printer. *Note:* Make sure that your printer is turned on and is
   connected to the computer.

Exercise 2: Using the Escape and Ctrl-C Keys to Stop a Command

This exercise demonstrates the difference between using the Escape
key and the Ctrl-C key combination to stop a command. This

exercise assumes that you have completed exercise 1. Follow these steps:

1. Type **dir** and press **Enter**. Notice the result of this command.

2. Again, type **dir** but instead of pressing Enter, press **Escape**.

    a. What effect does this action have on the DIR command?

    b. Were the results the same as in step 1 above? Why?

3. At the DOS prompt, type **dir** again, press **Enter**, and *very quickly* press the **Ctrl-C** key combination.

    a. What effect does this action have on the DIR command?

    b. How does it differ from pressing Escape?

4. Try pausing the result of the DIR command by typing **dir** again, pressing **Enter**, and *very quickly* pressing the **Pause** button (located in the upper right portion of your keyboard).

    a. What effect does this action have on the DIR command?

    b. How does it differ from pressing Escape and Ctrl-C?

5. Make a short list of when you might use each of these key combinations.

Exercise 3: More Practice Using Wildcards with the DIR Command

In this exercise, you practice using the ? and * wildcards with the DIR command. The exercise also assumes that you are using a computer with a hard disk designated as Drive C:, that Drive C: is the default drive, and that you have a subdirectory named \DOS on that drive. It assumes that you are starting from the root directory of Drive C:. Follow these steps:

1. Type **dir** and press **Enter**. Make a note of how many files are listed and what they are.

2. Type **dir c:\dos** and press **Enter**. Try to stop the screen from scrolling. (*Hint:* You can stop the scrolling in four ways.) Press the **F3** key, and then press **Enter** to repeat the command until you have practiced all four of the ways to stop the screen from scrolling.

    a. How many total files were listed?

    b. Were there more files or fewer files than what was listed in step 1?

3. Type **dir c:\dos\c*.*** and press **Enter**.

    a. Did you notice a difference in the file listings compared to what you received in step 2? (**Hint:** All the listed files start with the letter *c* in this step.)

    b. How many total files were listed?

4. Type **dir c:\dos\c*** and press **Enter**.

    a. Did you remember to use the F3 key to repeat the part of the previous command that applies in this step?

    b. How did the results compare to the previous results of the DIR command?

    c. How many total files were listed?

5. Make the DOS directory the default directory by typing **cd \dos** and pressing **Enter**. You will learn more about this command later in the book.

6. Type **dir c*** and press **Enter**.

    a. Were the results the same as you received in steps 3 and 4?

    b. How many total files were listed? Make a note of the similarities and differences between each of these commands, and be sure you understand them before moving on.

7. Type **dir c*.** and press **Enter**. (**Hint:** Don't forget to type the "dot" after the "star" in this command.)

    a. Were the results the same as you received in steps 3, 4, and 6?

    b. How many total files were listed? Make a note of the similarities and differences between each of these commands, and be sure you understand them before moving on.

Exercise 4: Using the DIR Command with Switches

In this exercise, you practice using the /w and /p switches with the
DIR command. Be sure that you understand each option and how it
affects the DIR command before moving on to the next step. This
exercise assumes that you are using a computer with a hard disk
designated as Drive C:, that Drive C: is the default drive, and you
have a subdirectory named \DOS on that drive. It also assumes that
you have completed exercise 3. Follow these steps:

1. Type **dir** and press **Enter**.

    a. How many total files were listed?

    b. Did they all appear on one screen?

    c. What information was displayed about each file?

2. Type **dir /w** (particularly note which way the slash goes) and
    press **Enter**.

    a. How many total files were listed?

    b. Did they all appear on one screen?

    c. What information was displayed about each file?

3. Type **dir /p** (particularly note which way the slash goes) and
    press **Enter**.

    a. How many total files were listed?

    b. Did they all appear on one screen? If not, how many
        screens were displayed?

    c. What information was displayed about each file?

4. Type **dir /b** (particularly note which way the slash goes) and
    press **Enter**.

    a. How many total files were listed?

    b. Did they all appear on one screen?

    c. What information was displayed about each file?

3

5. Type **dir /on** (particularly note which way the slash goes) and press **Enter**.

    a. How many total files were listed?

    b. Did they all appear on one screen?

    c. What information was displayed about each file?

    d. What order were they displayed in?

6. Type **dir /os** (particularly note which way the slash goes) and press **Enter**.

    a. How many total files were listed?

    b. Did they all appear on one screen?

    c. What information was displayed about each file?

    d. What order were they displayed in?

7. Type **dir /oe** (particularly note which way the slash goes) and press **Enter**.

    a. How many total files were listed?

    b. Did they all appear on one screen?

    c. What information was displayed about each file?

    d. What order were they displayed in?

8. Type **dir /od** (particularly note which way the slash goes) and press **Enter**.

    a. How many total files were listed?

    b. Did they all appear on one screen?

    c. What information was displayed about each file?

    d. What order were they displayed in?

9. Type **dir /p/w** (particularly note which way each slash goes) and press **Enter**.

    a. How many total files were listed?

    b. Did they all appear on one screen? If not, how many screens were displayed?

    c. What information was displayed about each file?

    d. How does this option compare to all of the previous options?

10. Type **dir /on/p/w** (particularly note which way each slash goes) and press **Enter**.

  a. How many total files were listed?

  b. Did they all appear on one screen? If not, how many screens were displayed?

  c. What information was displayed about each file?

  d. Was this any different than step 4?

  e. How does this option compare to all of the previous options?

Exercise 5: Using the Help Command

In this exercise, you practice using the DOS HELP command. The exercise assumes that you are using a computer with a hard disk designated as Drive C:, that Drive C: is the default drive, that you have a subdirectory named \DOS on that drive, and that you have made the \DOS subdirectory the default. If you are using a network system, you will need to change to the DOS subdirectory before continuing. Follow these steps:

1. At the DOS command line, type **help dir** and press **Enter**. Notice what appears on-screen.

2. Print the screen contents by pressing **Shift-PrtScn**. *Note:* Make sure that your printer is turned on before entering the command and is connected to the computer.

3. Type **dir /?** and press **Enter**. Is the information displayed the same as before?

4. Print the screen contents by pressing **Shift-PrtScn,** and compare the results to what you received in step 2. Were they the same?

5. How many options are presented in the help screens? Try any options you have not already practiced.

Continuing Problems

Each of the following case studies is continued throughout the rest of the book. This section describes each scenario; the information provided here applies to all the other problems in which the respective case studies appear.

Case Study 1: Burke's Musical Instruments

Case Study 1 involves Burke's Musical Instruments, a family-owned specialty business that sells musical instruments and rents them to elementary and high school students. When the business first began two years ago, owner Debbie Burke did all record keeping manually. The business quickly became a tremendous success. Debbie had to hire one full-time employee, Pamela Oropeza, and two part-time employees, Issa Freeman and Shinichi Murakami, to assist with orders, inventory, and the transition to automating her business records and transactions. She recently purchased a computer system. She is reading all the computer books she can get her hands on, but she is finding out that there is more to learn about computers than she originally thought.

Debbie has been learning the commands that came with the MS-DOS operating system but has frequently been getting the message Bad command or file name. She realizes that she will eventually become more familiar with the proper syntax, but finds it frustrating to have to look up each command in the system documentation book when she needs help. Debbie wants to access on-line help because it would be more convenient. Is there anything Debbie can do to help herself as she becomes more familiar with the DOS commands? List the various ways she might access the MS-DOS on-line help system.

Case Study 2: Medical Offices of Colby, Odenthal, Bravo & Kim

Case Study 2 involves the medical offices of Colby, Odenthal, Bravo & Kim. The firm recently purchased a dozen new personal computers for the staff. All tasks that previously were done manually will now be done using a computer. They received the first computer and began training the employees. Doctors Christina Colby and Lisa

Odenthal used computers when they were in college, but Doctors Patricia Bravo and Su-Jin Kim have never touched one before now. Because everybody's computer experience is relatively limited, they have been all learning DOS on their own up until now.

The administrative assistant, Richard Bess, is experimenting with the DIR command and learning how it works. From within the DOS directory, he wants to list all the files that begin with the letters DISK and end with the COM extension. Execute the command on your computer and print a hard copy of what is displayed.

Case Study 3: The DOS Reference Card

Case Study 3 involves creating a DOS reference card. You will encounter many commands, terms, and key sequences when you are using MS-DOS 6.2. This case study emphasizes the key points introduced in previous chapters. In the blanks in the following list, write the command, term, or key sequence that matches each description. You will add to this DOS reference card throughout the book.

Description	Command/Term/Sequence	Type
A place for temporary storage of programs and data while the computer is running.	_____	Term
The software that provides the basic functional link between DOS and the peripheral hardware in a PC.	_____	Term
Interprets what you type, and processes input so that DOS can take the appropriate action.	_____	Command
Stops commands in which DOS pauses for you to type more information.	_____	Sequence
Performs a warm boot.	_____	Sequence

(continues)

Description	Command/Term/Sequence	Type
Displays a command's syntax or an overview of all DOS commands.	_____	Command
Provides a list of files, the date and time of each creation, and the sizes.	_____	Command
Enables you to reuse DOS commands more easily at the command line.	_____	Command
The ? character matches any single character in that position, and the * character matches all characters in that part of the full file name.	_____	Term

 Challenge Problems

1. How can you list your files by date and time order?

2. Pressing the F3 key copies all remaining characters from the last command executed. How can you recall the command executed before that?

Answers to Odd-Numbered Questions

Key Term Matching Questions

1. c	11. e
3. f	13. j
5. k	15. l
7. t	17. n
9. r	19. i

Multiple-Choice Questions

1.	e	7.	e
3.	c	9.	a
5.	d		

True/False Questions

1.	F	7.	F
3.	T	9.	T
5.	F		

3

Using the DOS Shell

Chapter Summary

Chapter 4 gets you up and running with the DOS Shell, exploring the DOS Shell screen and discussing aspects of the Shell common to all its commands. The DOS Shell is a mildly controversial feature of DOS, praised by some as an easier way of using DOS, derided by others as a crutch. The DOS Shell has features that are strikingly familiar to Windows users with a point-and-click interface, disks and directories displayed in tree format, and the capability of associating file name extensions with the program that produced them.

One thing is certain: the DOS Shell adds a new dimension to using DOS. Even if you are comfortable using DOS at the DOS prompt, you should explore the DOS Shell. Important points covered in Chapter 4 include the following:

- The DOS Shell provides a visual interface that enables you to operate your computer quickly and easily without having to type commands at the DOS prompt.

- You can use the DOS Shell without a mouse, but using a mouse or other pointing device makes your actions go quickly, easily, and intuitively.

- Windows users may find many of the keystrokes and features of the DOS Shell to be familiar.

- You access DOS Shell features through a menu. When you choose the main menu prompts, a pull-down menu containing that menu's options appears.

- Some options in the DOS Shell's menus display a dialog box to enable you to specify parameters and options needed for the option.

- The DOS Shell's Task Swapper enables you to move easily from program to program with just a few keystrokes.

- You can associate programs with their data files, and you can start programs using hot keys.

- You can add or change the program groups and program items that appear in the Shell's program list area.

- You can use the Shell to manipulate files and directories quickly and easily.

Chapter Outline

I. What is the DOS Shell?

II. Starting the DOS Shell

    A. Using the Shell Interface
    B. Selecting an Area
    C. Moving Around an Area

III. Using the DOS Shell Menus

    A. Using the Menu Bar
    B. Using Pull-Down Menus
    C. Using Keystroke Commands
    D. Using Dialog Boxes
    E. Modifying the View

IV. Using the Shell Screen Modes

V. Using the Help System

VI. Using the Program List

    A. Working with Program Groups
    B. Working with Program Items

VII. Working with Directories and Files

     A. Expanding and Collapsing Branches
     B. Creating Directories

VIII. Selecting Files in the DOS Shell

     A. Selecting a Single File
     B. Selecting Multiple Files
     C. Selecting All Files
     D. Deselecting All Files
     E. Selecting Files across Directories

IX. Using the Shell to View a File

X. Associating Files with Programs

XI. Using the Task Swapper

XII. Copying Files in the Shell

XIII. Moving a File in the Shell

Active Learning

Key Term Matching

Match the following key terms with the definitions listed after them.

____ 1. Selection cursor		____ 11. Double-click
____ 2. Mouse pointer		____ 12. Program group
____ 3. F1		____ 13. Keys
____ 4. GUI		____ 14. Command button
____ 5. Task swapping		____ 15. Shell
____ 6. Escape		____ 16. Index
____ 7. Program item		____ 17. F10
____ 8. List box		____ 18. Dialog boxes
____ 9. Mouse driver		____ 19. F9
____ 10. F3		____ 20. Scroll bar

4

Definitions

a. Cancels a pulled-down menu while maintaining an active menu bar so that you can select another menu name.

b. A dialog box that contains information or a list of choices displayed in a rectangular area.

c. Starts a specific software application on your hard disk.

d. A form of interface that provides icons to indicate single programs and groups.

e. A rounded-rectangular button, usually found near the bottom edge of a dialog box.

f. A program that acts as a user interface to the features and capabilities of an operating system.

g. This command button at the bottom of a help screen displays an index of help information on keystroke commands.

h. An area of the screen containing arrows and icons that serve to move the items through the window.

i. Cancels a pulled-down menu without making a selection, returning to the preceding window display.

j. An area of highlighted text that shows where selected action occurs.

k. A program that routinely displays messages and prompts in pop-up boxes on-screen.

l. Displays context-sensitive help in DOS Shell.

m. Pressing the left mouse button twice in rapid succession.

n. The block- or arrow-shaped screen icon that indicates where the mouse action occurs.

o. This key views file contents using the DOS Shell.

p. A technique that gives the DOS Shell the capacity to load more than one program at a time.

q. A program that must be loaded into memory to operate a mouse.

r. This command button (located on the bottom of a help screen) displays the DOS Shell help index, a list of topics on which you can receive help.

s. Pressing this key exits the DOS Shell, returns to the command line, and removes the DOS Shell from memory.

t. A collection of program items; these enable you to group your applications by category.

Multiple-Choice Questions

____ 1. Which DOS Shell keystroke command repaints the screen?

    a. F7
    b. F8
    c. F5
    d. F9
    e. F3

____ 2. In text mode, all screen presentation is composed of ____ characters.

    a. bit-mapped
    b. ASCII
    c. ANSI
    d. POST
    e. hexadecimal

____ 3. Which DOS Shell keystroke command activates the menu bar?

    a. F8
    b. F5
    c. F3
    d. F10
    e. F1

____ 4. A dialog box that contains information or a list of choices displayed in a rectangular area is referred to as a

    a. list box.
    b. option button.
    c. text box.
    d. selection box.
    e. check box.

4

____ 5. The option of seeing two file lists on the same DOS Shell
screen is called

    a. Two Lists.
    b. Double File Lists.
    c. Double Lists.
    d. Single File Lists.
    e. Dual File Lists.

____ 6. The DOS Shell provides many keystroke command
shortcuts, called

    a. Shellstrokes.
    b. hot keys.
    c. hot shells.
    d. Alt keys.
    e. Control keys.

____ 7. When you work with the DOS Shell, the program routinely
displays messages and prompts in pop-up boxes, called
____ boxes, on-screen.

    a. graphics
    b. icon
    c. menu
    d. dialog
    e. text

____ 8. Which of the following is not a command button contained
in most DOS Shell dialog boxes?

    a. OK
    b. Cancel
    c. Quit
    d. Help
    e. All of these answers are valid command buttons.

____ 9. At any time during a DOS Shell session, pressing ____
causes a help window to appear.

    a. Ctrl-H
    b. Enter
    c. Alt-F10
    d. F1
    e. Ctrl-F1

____10. When you first install the DOS Shell, the program list area lists the program group called

      a. Word Processing.
      b. QBasic.
      c. Database.
      d. Programs.
      e. Main.

True/False Questions

____ 1. The first time you start the DOS Shell, the window displays the directory tree area, the file list area, and the program list area.

____ 2. The DOS Shell can be used to view file lists and file contents but not to run programs.

____ 3. Using the F3 key alone or pressing Alt-F4 exits the DOS Shell and removes it from memory.

____ 4. Dialog boxes fall into two general categories: those that request information and those that provide information.

____ 5. The top line of the DOS Shell window is the status line.

____ 6. Like Windows, the DOS Shell was built to be used as a graphical interface.

____ 7. When you install DOS 6.2, you are prompted for whether you want the DOS Shell to be started automatically.

____ 8. Many support consultants find that if they teach new users the ins and outs of the DOS Shell, they end up fielding fewer support calls from inexperienced users.

____ 9. The DOS Shell allows you to display several active windows at a time.

____10. You can initiate virtually every DOS Shell operation by choosing options from menus.

4

Directed Exercises

For all of these exercises, you will be using the DOS Shell. Start the DOS Shell by typing **dosshell** at the command prompt and then pressing **Enter**. These exercises assume that you are using a mouse. If you don't have a mouse, you must press Enter or the F10 key to perform an action; the arrow and Tab keys to move from window to window; and the Alt key to activate a menu from the menu bar. The term *click* refers to moving the mouse pointer to an option and quickly pressing and releasing the left mouse button; or using the arrow keys, you can move the selection cursor to an option and press Enter or the F10 key.

Exercise 1: Working in the DOS Shell Window

In this exercise, you learn the parts of the DOS Shell window. Follow these steps:

1. Locate the menu bar, drive letter, area title bar, status line, scroll bars, title bar, and mouse pointer (if you are using a mouse).

2. Click the drive letter C, listed below the menu bar. The left window titled Directory Tree lists all directories that are contained on Drive C:. Click the DOS directory to see what effect it has on the right window.

3. Use the scroll down arrow, located on the right side of the right window, to move down one line at a time. Move the mouse pointer off the arrow and position in on the scroll bar. Press the left mouse button. The screen scrolls one page at a time. Position the mouse pointer on the scroll box, press and hold the left mouse button, and drag down the scroll box. What effect does this dragging action have?

4. Move the mouse pointer to the left window and press the left mouse button. What actions can you perform in this window?

Exercise 2: Using the DOS Shell

This exercise uses an Activities disk. If you are using a networked system, your instructor will provide information on how to obtain or create this disk. This book occasionally asks you to use an Activities disk to perform exercises. Follow these steps:

1. Click the drive letter A to display the contents of the Activities disk. Click the CHAP4 directory. What file name is listed, and when was the file created?

2. With the Activities disk in Drive A: and the DOS Shell displaying the contents of CHAP4 directory from the Activities disk, execute the TESTME.BAT file. What message is displayed? What type of action did you perform?

3. From the File menu, choose Copy. The Copy File dialog box appears and prompts you to enter a file name.

4. Enter **NEWTEST.BAT**, and click the OK button. Notice that the new file is created in the CHAP4 directory. This file is an exact duplicate of TESTME.BAT.

5. Choose Options from the menu bar. Click the Confirmation option. A dialog box appears with three confirmation choices. These choices enable you to turn on or off message boxes relating to these options. The other options listed enable you to change the display information, screen colors, and display modes.

6. Choose View from the menu bar. Click the Dual File Lists option. Choose View from the menu bar, and click the Single File List option. Notice the difference between the two options. Click the other selections to see the differences for each menu selection.

7. Choose Tree from the menu bar. Select each option, and note how the directory listings change. The tree enables you to expand subdirectories for the current drive selected.

8. Choose Help from the menu bar. At any time during a DOS Shell session, press the **F1** key to activate the on-line Help system. The Help menu shows different choices, depending on the type of help you require. The most common option used is Index. This option produces a list of indexed topics for each menu bar option. To exit a Help topic, press **Escape** or choose the Close command button to return to the screen from which you activated Help.

4

Exercise 3: Creating and Modifying a Program Group

In this exercise, you practice creating and modifying a program group, adding it to your DOS Shell interface. Follow these steps:

1. To add a new program group, make the program list area the active area of the DOS Shell window and display the Main program group by pressing **Escape** as many times as necessary until the title bar of the program list area displays the title Main.

2. Use the mouse or cursor-movement keys to select the intended "parent" group (Main) in the program list area.

3. When the Main program group is highlighted, choose New from the **F**ile menu. The New Program Object dialog box appears, containing two option buttons for Program Group and Program Item.

4. Click the Program Group option button, and then click the OK command button or press **Enter**.

5. The Add Group dialog box appears, containing three text boxes for Title, Help Text, and Password. Type the words **Practice Applications** in the Title text box. (*Note:* This title appears not only in the program list area, but also in that area's title bar when a program group is activated.)

6. Press **Tab** to move to the Help Text box, then type a help message of up to 255 characters. Type **Displays practice applications** in the box, noting that only 20 characters appear at a time in the text box.

7. Press **Tab** to move to the Password box, then type your first name in the Password text box to limit access to a DOS Shell program group.

8. Click the OK command button or press **Enter**. The Shell adds the new program group to the selected program group.

9. To change your newly-created program group's properties, highlight the group's name in the file list area and choose **Prop**erties from the **F**ile menu. The Program Group Properties dialog box appears. When prompted to enter a password, type the password you entered in Step 7.

10. This dialog box is essentially a copy of the Add Group dialog box, except that everything you already entered for the selected group already appears in the text boxes. Verify that the entries are what you typed in the previous steps.

11. Change the password by entering your last name (instead of your first name, used previously), and then click OK or press **Enter**.

Exercise 4: Adding a Program Item

In this exercise, you practice adding a program item to your new program group created in exercise 3. Adding a program item is similar to adding a program group. Follow these steps:

1. To add a new program group, make the program list area the active area of the DOS Shell window and then highlight the Practice Applications program group, created in exercise 3. (Press **Escape** until Main appears in the title bar of the program list and then use the mouse or cursor-movement keys to highlight *Practice Applications*.)

2. After you select the program group, choose New from the File menu, and choose Program Item from the dialog box. The Add Program dialog box appears.

3. Select the Program Title text box and type the words **Practice Program** in the box.

4. Select the Command text box and enter the name of a command. Either use a command supplied by your instructor, or type the command **chkdsk**.

5. Select the Startup Directory text box and enter the name of the directory where the command entered in step 4 resides. If you selected the CHKDSK command, enter **c:\dos** in this box.

6. Click on the OK button when your entry is complete.

7. Test your Program Item by highlighting the Practice Program item and double-clicking the mouse, or press **Enter** to execute the command. Did it work? How does this compare to entering commands from the DOS prompt?

4

Exercise 5: Managing Directories by Using the DOS Shell

This exercise concentrates on managing directories using the DOS Shell. It includes selecting, expanding, collapsing, creating, changing, and removing directories. To successfully complete this exercise, make sure that you insert the Activities disk into the appropriate disk drive. The drive area at the top of the DOS Shell window highlights the selected drive icon. Follow these steps:

1. Using the DOS Shell, change the drive icon to display the directory tree for the Activities disk. Select the CHAP4 directory.

2. Show the directory tree for the Activities disk by selecting the appropriate drive icon. Print a hard copy of the screen display.

3. Show the directory tree for Drive C:. Print a hard copy of the screen display.

4. Show a directory tree both for Drive C: and for the Activities disk. *Hint:* You will need to change the way the DOS Shell views multiple directories.

5. Using the DOS Shell, change the drive icon to display the directory tree for the Activities disk.

6. Expand the directory listing to display all subdirectories. *Hint:* Look for the plus (+) sign in the directory tree window.

7. After you expand the root directory of the Activities disk, are there any other plus (+) signs listed with any subdirectories? How can you expand all directories and their subdirectories?

8. The directories now are expanded. Collapse the directories so that only the root directory appears.

9. Create a new subdirectory called NEW_1. This directory should be a subdirectory of the CHAP4 directory. Copy the TEST1.FIL file into the NEW_1 subdirectory from the CHAP4 directory.

10. Create another subdirectory called NEW_2, as a subdirectory of CHAP4. Print a hard copy of the screen display. Copy all files with the FIL extension into the NEW_1 subdirectory from the CHAP4 directory.

11. Change to the NEW_1 directory. Are there any files listed within this directory?

12. Change to the NEW_2 directory. Are there any files listed within this directory? Are there any subdirectories of NEW_2?

13. Make CHAP4 the current directory and rename NEW_2 to NEW_02. Print a hard copy of the screen display.

14. Remove the NEW_02 directory. You can remove a directory while using the DOS Shell in two ways. Can you name them? Remove the NEW_1 directory. What should you do first before you remove the directory?

15. Delete the program group/items that you created by highlighting them and then pressing **Delete**.

Continuing Problems

Each of the following case studies began in Chapter 3 and continues throughout the rest of the book. Refer to Chapter 3 for a description of each case study.

Case Study 1: Burke's Musical Instruments

Debbie Burke and her full-time employee Pamela Oropeza have become fairly proficient using the commands that came with the MS-DOS operating system but they want to spare Issa and Shinichi the problems they had during the learning process. Is there anything they can show the part-time employees to make it easier until they become more familiar with the DOS commands? Make a list of all the things they might be able to do with the DOS Shell.

Case Study 2: Medical Offices of Colby, Odenthal, Bravo & Kim

Dr. Kim has not had much time to practice with the computer because she has been extremely busy with her patients. However, she really needs to access various commands and programs on the computer, so administrative assistant Richard Bess has decided to make it easier for her. List the steps he must take to add three program groups with two program items each. What program groups and

4

items might be likely to exist in a medical practice. Practice creating similar program groups and items, using programs that currently exist on your computer, and then execute each of the commands on your computer.

Case Study 3: The DOS Reference Card

Case Study 3 involves creating a DOS reference card. You will encounter many commands, terms, and key sequences when you are using MS-DOS 6.2. This case study emphasizes the key points introduced in previous chapters. In the blanks in the following list, write the command, term, or key sequence that matches each description. You will add to this DOS reference card throughout the book.

Description	Command/Term/Sequence	Type
A visually oriented user interface that replaces the DOS command line with easy-to-use menus.	_____	Command
A keystroke command shortcut.	_____	Term
Graphical User Interface	_____	Term

 # Challenge Problems

1. Thu-Thuy Pham needs to create a specified shortcut-key combination to start her word processing program. What three conditions must be met before a "hot key" can start the program?

2. Working with a partner, activate the Windows program on one computer and activate the DOS Shell on another. Compare the two interfaces and make a list of the differences and similarities between them.

Answers to Odd-Numbered Questions

Key Term Matching Questions

1. j	11. m
3. l	13. g
5. p	15. f
7. c	17. a
9. q	19. o

Multiple-Choice Questions

1. c	7. d
3. d	9. d
5. e	

True/False Questions

1. T	7. T
3. T	9. F
5. F	

4

Data Files to Active Learning

Exercise	Beginning Name	Ending Name
Directed Exercise		
2	TESTME.BAT	NEWTEST.BAT
5	TEST1.FIL TEST2.FIL	TEST1.FIL TEST2.FIL

Understanding Files and Directories

Chapter Summary

Chapter 5 is the first of seven chapters that cover everything you need to know about the "heart" of DOS, including working with disks and the files stored on them. This chapter recognizes the important job DOS performs in managing your files, defines files, and clearly explains file-naming conventions. It also explores the tree-structure directory system used by DOS to organize files as well as commands that create, change, remove, and display directories.

Chapter 5 covers the following key points about DOS file requirements and directories:

- DOS organizes files into a file system that DOS manages.

- Disks are the main storage medium for DOS-based PCs.

- Files are the storage units of disks.

- File names consist of name portions (up to eight characters to the left of the period) and extensions (up to three characters to the right of the period).

- File name characters must be "legal" to DOS.

- DOS tracks file names in a disk directory. Each file name in a directory must be unique.

- By convention, certain file names refer to specific types of files. You can override file-naming conventions, but observing these conventions makes file names more meaningful.

- DOS uses one of its standard devices when you use a file name that contains the device names. Avoid using the names PRN, CON, NUL, LPT, and COM in file names.

- Directories organize files and are a primary management tool you can use to make your work productive.

- The primary commands for working with directories are MD (create a directory), CD (change to a directory), and RD (remove a directory).

- You can rename a directory by using the MOVE command.

- A path is a unique address that identifies where a file is located. The path is composed of all the directories that must be traversed to reach a given file.

- The PATH command can help you access commonly used programs.

- The TREE command helps you get a better picture of your directory structure.

Chapter Outline

I. Introducing the DOS File System

    A. Understanding Files
    B. Understanding File Names
    C. Observing File-Naming Conventions
    D. Avoiding Bad File Names
    E. Understanding File Attributes

II. Understanding the Role of Directories

III. Expanding the File System through Subdirectories

    A. Understanding Path Name Expressions
    B. Creating Directories with MKDIR (MD)
    C. Changing the current Directory with CHDIR (CD)

D. Deleting Directories with RMDIR (RD)
E. Using DELTREE to Delete Directories
F. Renaming Directories

IV. Helping DOS Find Files with PATH

V. Listing Directories with TREE

VI. Using a Temporary Directory

Active Learning

Key Term Matching

Match the following key terms with the definitions listed after them.

_____ 1. Root directory

_d_ 2. File Allocation Table

_g_ 3. TREE

_t_ 4. RD

_____ 5. Path name expression

_a_ 6. File attribute

_e_ 7. Logical device

_b_ 8. PATH

_h_ 9. Read-only

_m_ 10. CON

_k_ 11. DELTREE

_g_ 12. Directory entry

_c_ 13. Extension

_n_ 14. Directory

_r_ 15. File name

_f_ 16. CD

_s_ 17. File

_i_ 18. PRN

_____ 19. Archive

_o_ 20. MD

Definitions

a. A file attribute that indicates a file has been altered or created since the last time the file was backed up.

b. Usually included as a statement in the AUTOEXEC.BAT file and determines where DOS can look on the system for program files.

c. Consists of up to three characters and traditionally describes the type of file or its format.

d. An important table created by the FORMAT command on every disk it touches, this table is the beginning of the disk's file system that is used to hold all files and directories.

e. DOS controls these by reserving a name to use as input or output parameters in a command line.

f. Changes to a new default directory.

g. Similar to a book's table of contents but stores information about the physical location of files on a disk.

h. A file attribute that indicates a file can be accessed for information but cannot be erased or modified with the COPY or REN commands.

i. A reserved device name that identifies a parallel printer port.

j. A variable length collection of related information that is referenced by a name.

k. This powerful command enables you to delete directories that contain files.

l. Indicates where DOS can find a specified file or group of files and is made up of three components: drives, directories, and files.

m. A reserved device name that identifies the screen and keyboard.

n. A "division" on a disk for the purpose of organizing your files.

o. This command is used to create a new directory on a disk.

p. A one-byte field in the directory entry that stores a number of characteristics about each file but is not displayed in a normal directory listing.

q. This external DOS command lists all the directories of a disk in their hierarchical structure.

r. Consists of one to eight characters followed by a period, usually providing a description of the contents of the file.

s. DOS tracks each file on a disk through one of these; it maintains critical information about the file and where it is stored on disk.

t. This command is used to remove an empty directory; it does not work if the directory contains files or has another directory branching from it.

Multiple-Choice Questions

_____ 1. The device name reserved by DOS to identify the screen and keyboard is:

      a. PRN
      b. LPT1
      c. COM
      d. NUL
      e. CON

_____ 2. All of the following characters are allowed in a file name or extension except

      a. - (hyphen)
      b. _ (underscore)
      c. (
      d. \
      e. 0

_____ 3. The maximum number of letters allowed in a file name (not counting the extension) is

      a. eight.
      b. three.
      c. five.
      d. eleven.
      e. six.

_____ 4. The DOS command that displays the full path as part of the DOS prompt is:

      a. PROMPT
      b. PATH
      c. ATTRIB
      d. MD
      e. AUTOEXEC.BAT

_____ 5. The command used to create a new directory or subdirectory is:

      a. CD
      b. RD
      c. MD
      d. CHDIR
      e. CREATE

5

____ 6. The ____ command deletes everything in its path regardless of file attributes.

    a. RD
    b. DELTREE
    c. DEL
    d. REM
    e. There is no such command in DOS 6.2.

____ 7. The DOS command that displays the hierarchical directory structure is:

    a. DIRTREE
    b. DIR /W
    c. DIR
    d. DISPLAY
    e. TREE

____ 8. The maximum number of characters that can be included in the PATH statement is

    a. 16.
    b. 8.
    c. 24.
    d. 127.
    e. 256.

____ 9. The directory automatically created by the DOS FORMAT command is:

    a. \DOS
    b. the root directory.
    c. a subdirectory.
    d. \KEEP
    e. There is no directory created by FORMAT.

____ 10. A common file name extension for a program file is:

    a. DAT
    b. COM
    c. BAT
    d. CFG
    e. BAK

True/False Questions

_____ 1. If you give a file name or extension too many characters, DOS issues a message warning that the file name and/or extension are too long.

_____ 2. The file name ME&YOU.US! is "legal" according to DOS rules.

_____ 3. Typing **DEL .** at the command line will have the same effect as typing **DEL *.*** at the command line.

_____ 4. DOS naming rules allow a directory name to be up to 11 characters long.

_____ 5. The DOS file name rules are only for floppy or hard disks and not for magnetic tape or CD ROMs.

_____ 6. DOS treats files ending with EXE and COM essentially the same.

_____ 7. DOS provides the external MKDIR command to create directories, but you can abbreviate the name of the command as MD for convenience.

_____ 8. Hidden files are listed by the DOS Shell in the file list area.

_____ 9. The name CLOCK$ is a DOS reserved name that cannot be used for a file name.

_____10. In order to use the DELTREE command to remove a directory, the directory must be completely empty.

▶ Directed Exercises

Exercise 1: Working with File Attributes

For this exercise, you need the Activities disk. Change to the CHAP5 subdirectory by typing **cd \chap5** from the drive where the disk is located. Follow these steps:

1. Set a read-only attribute for the TEST.FIL file.

2. You have two ways to check to see whether the attribute is in effect without using the DEL command. What are they?

5

3. Delete the TEST.FIL file by typing **del test.fil** and pressing **Enter**. What message is displayed? If you did not get a message, did you perform step 2?

4. Another file on the Activities disk is called TEST3.FIL. Did you see this file? This file is a hidden file. Display this file by using the ATTRIB command. Print a hard copy of the screen display.

5. Without changing the file attribute on TEST3.FIL, delete the file by typing **del test3.fil** and pressing **Enter**. What message is displayed? Why? No read-only attribute is assigned.

6. Remove the read-only attribute on the TEST.FIL file. Print a hard copy of the screen display.

7. Start the DOS Shell and place a read-only attribute on TEST3.FIL.

8. Replace the read-only attribute on TEST3.FIL with a hidden attribute.

9. Change the hidden attribute on TEST3.FIL to read-only.

10. Remove the read-only attribute for TEST3.FIL.

11. Change the read-only attribute on TEST3.FIL to hidden.

12. Print a hard copy of the screen display.

Exercise 2: Using the PATH Command

This exercise demonstrates how a search path operates and what is involved in creating and using the PATH command. Follow these steps, and answer each question:

1. At the DOS prompt, type **cd ** and press **Enter**. The directory changes to the root directory.

2. Type **help path** and press **Enter**. Does the Help information for the PATH command display?

3. At the DOS prompt, type **path ;** and press **Enter**.

4. Again, type **help path** and press **Enter**. Does the Help information for the PATH command display? Did it work in step 1? Why doesn't it work now?

5. At the DOS prompt, type **path** and press **Enter**. What message appears? What effect did the semicolon in step 2 have on the PATH command?

6. At the DOS prompt, type **path c:\dos** and press **Enter**.

7. Once again, type **help path** and press **Enter**. Does the Help information for the PATH command display? Why does it work this time, but not in step 2?

8. This question is somewhat challenging. Because you changed the search path to search only the current directory and the DOS directory, how can you reset the path to the way it was before you changed it?

Exercise 3: File-Naming Conventions

A list of file names follows. Are these names valid according to file-naming conventions? If not, why?

filenames.1

FILENAMES.1

testthis.FIL

1234_.who

newltr.memo

copy?me.dos

README.DOC

(Rb_001).$$$

dos 5.0

me/you.doc

another,ltr

READ.ME

iStHisa.fil

<new>.TXT

helP.eXe

5

Exercise 4: Managing Directories from the DOS Command Line

For this exercise, you will practice creating, changing, removing, and displaying directories by using the DOS command line. Insert the Activities disk into the appropriate disk drive. Change to the drive where the Activities disk resides by typing the drive letter and a colon (:) and then pressing **Enter**. Follow these steps:

1. Create a subdirectory under the CHAP5 directory called NEW_1A. You can use MD NEW_1A if the current directory is CHAP5.

2. Create another subdirectory under CHAP5 called NEW_2A. Make sure that the printer is on, and then type **tree > prn** and press **Enter**.

3. Change to the NEW_2A directory. If you want to change to the NEW_1A directory, what full DOS command would you use? Can you use CD NEW_1A and why? What would happen if you executed the command CD \ from the DOS command line?

4. Change to the CHAP5 directory. What does the DOS prompt look like?

5. Copy the file TEST.FIL from the CHAP5 directory into the NEW_1A directory. Verify that TEST.FIL does exist in the NEW_1A directory. What command do you use to verify that the file truly does exist in the NEW_1A directory?

6. Remove the NEW_1 directory. What DOS message appears? What should you do before removing a subdirectory that contains data files? Remove the NEW_2 directory.

7. From the DOS command line, issue the TREE command to display all directories on the hard disk.

8. Using the TREE command from Drive C:, display the tree structure for the Activities disk.

9. Using the TREE command from Drive C:, display all files in all directories of the Activities disk and redirect the output to the printer.

Continuing Problems

Refer to the complete description of the case studies in Chapter 3.

Case Study 1: Burke's Musical Instruments

Shinichi Murakami turned on his computer just as he does any other day. Normally, to start the word processing software, he enters **wp** at the DOS prompt. Today, however, instead of the word processor appearing on-screen, he saw the DOS error message Bad command or file name. He tried entering **wp** again, but the same Bad command or file name message appeared. What could be the problem? How can he solve this problem?

Case Study 2: Medical Offices of Colby, Odenthal, Bravo & Kim

Secretary Claudia Ramirez was writing a business letter with her favorite word processing package. She attempted to save her file as BUSINESS.LTR, and got a message telling her that access is denied. She decided to save the file to another name and exit the software. At the DOS prompt, she listed the directory and to her surprise BUSINESS.LTR was not listed. What would cause the error message, and why couldn't she save her file under that name?

Ivan Dasilva, one of the part-time employees, has begun converting some of your manual data to automated computer files. He gives you a disk containing various files. He informs you that the important and necessary files have DBF and NDX extensions. What software application(s) uses these files?

Case Study 3: The DOS Reference Card

In this case study, you continue creating the DOS reference card you began in Chapter 5. Several terms and DOS commands are introduced in this chapter and should be added to the reference card. Fill in the command, term, or key sequence that matches each description.

5

Description	Command/Term/Sequence	Type
The command that enables you to assign an attribute to a file.		Command
A master directory created by the FORMAT command.		Term
A command that enables DOS to locate and execute program files with COM, EXE, and BAT extensions.		Command
A command that enables you to change the DOS prompt.		Command
Sending the output or input of a command to a device other than the standard input or output.		Term
Changes the current directory or shows the path of the current directory.		Command
Removes a subdirectory that contains files.		Command
Removes an empty subdirectory.		Command
Creates a subdirectory.		Command
Displays all subdirectories on a disk or, optionally, lists all files in each subdirectory.		Command

 # Challenge Problems

1. With today's large hard disks and numerous software applications that perform different functions, you could overrun the 127-character limit for the PATH command.

   a. Is there a way to overcome this limitation?

   b. If so, how?

2. Ken Fry recently bought a new computer with preloaded software. His computer contains many directories and subdirectories used by the various software applications. Not knowing the specifics of the different software applications, how can he display a listing of all files in all directories?

3. Noreth Men's current working directory is C:\FILES\MEMOS. She is cleaning up her hard disk by deleting old files. She removes the files that are old and not worth keeping, and moves the files that she wants to keep to a floppy disk. The MEMOS directory is empty (contains no data files), so she decides to remove the MEMOS directory. At the DOS command line, she types **rd memos** and presses **Enter**, but she receives the DOS error message `Invalid path, not directory, or directory not empty`. She checked for files using the DIR command with the /A switch and found no files.

   a. Why can't she remove the MEMOS directory?

   b. Why would she use the /A switch with the DIR command?

4. In order to see how his hard disk is organized, Martin Chavez executes the TREE command, and the screen scrolls; now he sees only the last part of the directories. The screen scrolled so so quickly that he could not see what was being displayed in the beginning. How can Martin view the tree structure one screen at a time?

Answers to Odd-Numbered Questions

Key Term Matching Questions

1.	d	11.	k
3.	q	13.	c
5.	l	15.	r
7.	e	17.	j
9.	h	19.	a

5

Multiple-Choice Questions

1.	e	7.	e
3.	a	9.	b
5.	c		

True/False Questions

1.	F	7.	F
3.	T	9.	T
5.	F		

Data Files to Active Learning

Exercise	Beginning Name	Ending Name
Directed Exercise		
1	TEST.FIL TEST3.FIL	TEST.FIL TEST3.FIL
5	TEST.FIL	TEST.FIL

Understanding Disks and Disk Drives

Chapter Summary

This chapter discusses how DOS stores information on your disk. You discover what disks are and learn about the different types of disks and drives. You learn how information is recorded on them, and some of the technological issues related to disks. Chapter 6 presents the following concepts:

- During formatting, DOS divides disks into tracks, cylinders, and sectors. A disk's storage capacity is governed by the number of sectors on the disk.

- Typical floppy-disk storage capacities are 360K, 720K, 1.2M, 1.44M, and 2.88M. Each floppy drive is designed to work optimally at one of these capacities.

- Hard disk capacities are determined by the number of platters and the number of sectors per track. Sectors, by default, hold 512 bytes of information.

Chapter Outline

I. Understanding the Disk's Magnetic Storage Technique

II. Understanding Disk Drives

    A. Hard Disk Drives
    B. Floppy Disk Drives
    C. Write-Protecting a Floppy Disk

III. Understanding the Dynamics of the Disk Drive

    A. Disk Drive Heads
    B. Disk Tracks
    C. Disk Cylinders
    D. Disk Sectors

IV. Understanding Disk Formats

    A. Floppy Disk Formats
    B. Raw Capacity and Usable Capacity
    C. Hard Disk Drive Formats

Active Learning

Key Term Matching

Match the following key terms with the definitions listed after them.

_____ 1. File allocation table   _____ 11. Write-protect tab

_____ 2. Cylinder   _____ 12. Formatting

_____ 3. Fixed disk   _____ 13. Kilobyte

_____ 4. Write-protect shutter   _____ 14. High-density

_____ 5. Disk tracks   _____ 15. Microfloppy

_____ 6. Megabyte   _____ 16. Read/write head

_____ 7. Minifloppy   _____ 17. Interleaving

_____ 8. Double-density   _____ 18. Disk drive

_____ 9. Platter   _____ 19. Gigabyte

_____ 10. File fragmentation   _____ 20. Sectors

Definitions

a. Thin stripes of magnetically recorded information placed in concentric circles on a disk.

b. The term for a billion bytes.

c. The density of drive technology brought in with the AT generation of computers, also known as "286" computers.

d. What happens to a file when it is too large to fit on one cylinder and ends up being written on widely dispersed cylinders.

e. Another name for the 5-1/4 inch flexible disk.

f. The alignment of heads on the same track position on different sides of the disk platters.

g. The part of the disk drive that magnetically records or reads magnetic particles in the oxide emulsion on a disk.

h. The term used to indicate a million bytes or characters of information.

i. A small sticky tape to put over the notch on a 5-1/4 inch diskette to prevent the disk drive from writing new information on it.

j. Areas that divide (or segment) tracks on a disk's surface; at the inside track, they are very close together, but at the outermost track the edges are spaced further apart.

k. When you delete a file, DOS simply changes this to mark as vacant the tracks and sectors that the file occupied.

l. This term refers to one thousand characters or bytes.

m. Another name for a hard disk.

n. A PC component made up of read/write heads, head-positioner mechanisms, and disk-spinning motors, which record data on disks.

o. The density of floppy disks common in the original PCs and XTs.

p. The term that describes a 3-1/2 inch mylar disk inside a rigid plastic case.

q. Typically expressed in a ratio that indicates how many sectors will be in between the first sector written and the next sector to be written.

r. One of these is a single ceramic or metal disk in a hard disk.

s. The process of preparing a new disk by placing a uniform pattern of information in all tracks of the disk, enabling DOS to slice each track into smaller, more manageable components.

t. A small plastic piece on the back of a 3-1/2 inch diskette that allows the drive to write on the disk when it is open and prevents writing when it is closed.

Multiple-Choice Questions

____ 1. The term that indicates a billion bytes is

    a. Megabyte.
    b. Terabyte.
    c. Gigabyte.
    d. Kilobyte.
    e. Billobyte.

____ 2. A circular section of a disk's surface that holds data is called a

    a. cylinder.
    b. sector.
    c. platter.
    d. diskette.
    e. track.

____ 3. The process DOS uses to prepare a disk to accept data is called

    a. formatting.
    b. sectoring.
    c. writing.
    d. partitioning.
    e. reading.

____ 4. A hard disk often contains multiple ____ which are arranged in a stack with space between them.

    a. sectors
    b. platters
    c. floppy disks
    d. tracks
    e. cylinders

_____ 5. A 5-1/4 inch, double-sided high-density diskette has a
capacity of

    a. 360K.
    b. 720K.
    c. 1.2M.
    d. 1.44M.
    e. 2.88M.

True/False Questions

_____ 1. High-density drives easily read and write double-density
disks, but double-density drives do not support high-
density disks.

_____ 2. The alignment of all heads on the same sector position on
different sides of the platters is called a cylinder.

_____ 3. DOS does not actually erase files, it just marks the tracks
and sectors as vacant.

_____ 4. To write-protect a 3-1/2 inch disk, locate the plastic write-
protect shutter and slide it so that the window is open.

_____ 5. At the inside track of a disk, sectors are very close
together, but at the outermost track, they are spaced
further apart.

▶ Directed Exercises

Exercise 1: Examining a Floppy Disk

Examine the physical characteristics of a floppy disk. You can perform certain safeguards on a floppy disk to prevent accidental file
deletion. Examine the 3 1/2-inch Activities disk. Locate the write-
protect source. Can you find the write-protect source on a 5 1/4-inch
floppy disk? On a 5 1/4-inch disk, notice the exposed portion of the
magnetic disk. Name five precautions to take when handling floppy
disks.

Exercise 2: Label the Components

Write the name of the component that matches each of the following
letter marking the illustrations.

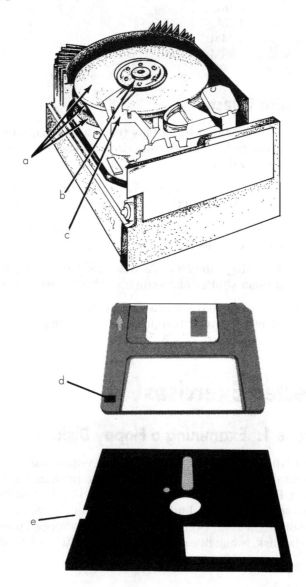

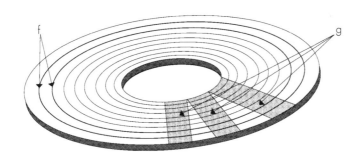

a. _____

b. _____

c. _____

d. _____

e. _____

f. _____

g. _____

Exercise 3: Research on Tracks and Sectors

Conduct a research project to discover how many tracks and sectors
are on each of the five floppy disk types: 5-1/4 inch double-density,
5-1/4 inch high-density, 3-1/2 inch double-density, 3-1/2 inch high-
density, and 3-1/2 inch extra high-density.

Answers to Odd-Numbered Questions

Key Term Matching Questions

1.	k	11.	i
3.	m	13.	l
5.	a	15.	p
7.	e	17.	q
9.	r	19.	b

Multiple-Choice Questions

1. c
3. a
5. c

True/False Questions

1. T
3. T
5. T

Preparing and Maintaining Disks

Chapter Summary

Chapter 7 builds on the information presented in the preceding chapters, explaining what formatting does and how DOS uses formatted disks to store files. It also covers how to partition a hard disk into sections that DOS can use as logical disks and how to use DOS commands to analyze disks for damage. The chapter covers the following key points:

- You must format both hard and floppy disks before you use them to store files.

- Formatting sets up a directory for file name and status information, and also creates a file-allocation table (FAT) that tracks the availability of storage space on the disk.

- Before you can format a hard disk, you must partition it by using FDISK.

- Disk partitions can be DOS partitions or partitions of another operating system.

- DOS partitions are either primary (bootable) partitions or extended partitions divided into one or more logical drives.

- The LABEL command adds or changes a disk's volume label.

- The VOL command displays a disk's volume label.

- You can use the SYS command to transfer system files to a floppy disk.

- CHKDSK is a disk-level command that finds and fixes problems. CHKDSK analyzes a disk's FAT and directory system.

- SCANDISK is an enhanced version of CHKDSK that works with both regular and DoubleSpace disk volumes.

Chapter Outline

I. Understanding Disk Preparation

II. Preparing Floppy Disks with the FORMAT Command

    A. Formatting Floppy Disks
    B. FORMAT's Other Tasks
    C. Using FORMAT's Switches

III. Preparing the Hard Disk

    A. Dividing a Hard Disk with FDISK
    B. Formatting a Hard Disk

IV. Related Commands

    A. Naming Disks with LABEL
    B. Examining Volume Labels with VOL
    C. Using SYS to Transfer the DOS System
    D. Analyzing a Disk with CHKDSK
    E. Analyzing a Disk with the ScanDisk Utility

Active Learning

Key Term Matching

Match the following key terms with the definitions listed after them.

____ 1. /V   ____ 11. CHKDSK

____ 2. Mirror image file   ____ 12. File Allocation Table

____ 3. System files   ____ 13. Logical Drive

____ 4. DoubleSpace   ____ 14. /S

____ 5. /Q   ____ 15. VOL

____ 6. LABEL   ____ 16. Format

____ 7. FDISK   ____ 17. Boot sector

____ 8. /ALL   ____ 18. Disk partition

____ 9. Cluster   ____ 19. Volume label

____ 10. /F:720   ____ 20. /U

Definitions

a. This switch instructs SCANDISK to check all local drives.

b. A partitioned section of a hard disk that DOS views as an additional hard disk.

c. A command that can be used to create disk partitions or display partition information.

d. When this switch is used with the FORMAT command, it copies the system files and COMMAND.COM to the formatted disk.

e. Hidden files stored in the boot sector of a disk; they can be transferred with the SYS command.

f. A division of a hard disk that DOS views as a separate disk.

g. When this switch is used with the FORMAT command, it formats a 3-1/2 inch double-density floppy disk in a high-density drive.

h. File-compression software that allocates storage in units smaller than a cluster.

i. Initial preparation of a disk for data storage.

j. When this switch is used with the FORMAT command, it performs an unconditional format so that the disk cannot be unformatted with UNFORMAT.

k. A DOS utility used to analyze a floppy or hard disk.

l. This file is created during the safe format procedure. It contains a copy of your hard disk's FAT, root directory, and boot record.

m. When this switch is used with the FORMAT command, it performs a quick format on a previously formatted disk.

n. A unit of one, four, or eight sectors; the smallest amount of disk space that DOS allocates to a file.

o. A DOS command used to display the volume label.

p. A name that identifies a particular disk.

q. When this switch is used with the CHKDSK command, it provides the file name on-screen while it analyzes the files.

r. A special disk table, always located on track 0, that logs every sector on a disk in units of one or more sectors.

s. A DOS command to add, modify, or change a volume label.

t. A special area in track 0 of each DOS disk used by DOS to record important information about a disk's format to reference later when working with the disk.

Multiple-Choice Questions

_____ 1. Which switch, when used with the FORMAT command, allocates space on the formatted disk for system files by creating hidden files of the same name and size on track 0?

    a. /F
    b. /B
    c. /Q
    d. /4
    e. /U

_____ 2. Which of the following is a character that could be used in a volume label?

    a. [
    b. >
    c. ,
    d. !
    e. ?

_____ 3. The _____ command detects and corrects problems in a DoubleSpace volume header.

    a. AUTOFIX
    b. CHKDSK
    c. CHKFIX
    d. SCANDISK
    e. SCANCHK

_____ 4. Which of the following DOS 6.2 FORMAT commands results in a bootable disk?

    a. FORMAT
    b. FORMAT /S
    c. FORMAT /B
    d. FORMAT /Q
    e. FORMAT /4

_____ 5. A _____ is an electronic identification on a disk, similar to a book title, that helps you identify the disk.

    a. format
    b. sector
    c. track
    d. volume label
    e. file name

_____ 6. Which switch formats a 5-1/4 inch 360K floppy disk in a high density drive when used with the FORMAT command?

    a. /1
    b. /8
    c. /4
    d. /6
    e. /9

____ 7. The command used to partition a hard disk is called:

   a. FDISK
   b. FORMAT
   c. PARTITION
   d. SECTOR
   e. PDISK

____ 8. The command used to add, modify, or change a disk's volume label is:

   a. VOL
   b. VER
   c. LABEL
   d. VOLUME
   e. CHKDSK

____ 9. The DOS command used to transfer system files to create a boot disk out of a data diskette is:

   a. COMMAND.COM
   b. SYS
   c. VOL
   d. VER
   e. FDISK

____ 10. A command that can be used to find and repair lost clusters is:

   a. FORMAT
   b. CLUSTER
   c. LABEL
   d. FDISK
   e. CHKDSK

True/False Questions

____ 1. CHKDSK is an enhanced version of SCANDSK that works with both regular and DoubleSpace disk volumes.

____ 2. A primary DOS partition is a bootable partition.

____ 3. The UNFORMAT command is used to restore a disk that has been formatted with the FORMAT /U command.

____ 4. The FDISK command does the same thing to hard disks that FORMAT does to floppy disks.

____ 5. The VOL command is used to add or change a disk's volume label.

____ 6. DOS views logical drives as being the same as physical drives and assigns each logical drive its own drive letter.

____ 7. You can use the SYS command to upgrade a disk's DOS version.

____ 8. When you use the /F switch with the CHKDSK command, the file names are displayed while the program analyzes the disk.

____ 9. Formatting a disk creates a File Allocation Table that tracks the availability of storage space on the disk.

____ 10. Disk partitions can be DOS partitions or partitions of another operating system.

▶ Directed Exercises

Exercise 1: Understanding the Format Command

What would happen if you executed the following commands? The A:\>, B:\>, or C:> indicates the default drive. Drive A: is a high-density 5 1/4-inch drive, and Drive B: is a high-density 3 1/2-inch drive.

1. C:\>FORMAT A: /S

2. C:\>FORMAT A: /F:360 /S

3. C:\>FORMAT

4. A:\>FORMAT A

5. A:\>FORMAT B: /F720 /V:DATA DISK

6. C:\>CHKDSK /F

7. C:\>VOL A:

8. C:\>LABEL A:SYS*DISK

9. A:\>CHKDSK B:

10. C:\>FORMAT B: /Q

11. A:\>FORMAT A: /S /V:SYS DISK /F:360

Exercise 2: Using the Format Command

In this exercise, you practice using the FORMAT command from the DOS Shell, and the DOS prompt from the DOS Shell and the DOS prompt. To complete this exercise, you need a blank floppy disk for Drive A: and access to the FORMAT command.

Beginning at the DOS Shell

1. Choose Format from the Main window.

2. A dialog box appears with Drive A: as the default. Why is the a: highlighted? What optional switch, if needed, would you use?

3. Press **Enter** to start the format process.

4. When prompted, insert a disk into Drive A:, and press **Enter**.

5. When prompted for a volume label, type the following:

    sys disk 6.0

6. When you return to the DOS Shell, exit and return to the DOS prompt. Type **vol a: > prn** and press **Enter**.

Beginning at the DOS Prompt

1. Type **format a: /s** and press **Enter**. If you have a double-density disk, you must also use the /F switch.

2. Insert a disk into Drive A: when prompted, and press **Enter**.

3. When prompted for a volume label, type the following:

    sys disk 6.0

Exercise 3: Transferring the System

In this exercise, you practice creating a DOS bootable system disk from a data disk. To complete this exercise, you can use the disk you formatted in exercise 2 or use a fresh disk. Follow these steps:

1. Format your disk as a data disk from either the DOS Shell or the DOS prompt. *(**Hint:** Do not use the /S switch.)*

2. Type **sys disk 6.0** for the volume label.

3. After you reformat the disk, see whether any files are stored on the disk by typing **dir a: /a** and pressing **Enter**. No files should be listed. You can print the listing by typing **dir*.* > prn** and pressing **Enter**.

4. Use the SYS command to transfer the system to the data disk in Drive A:. Use the DIR command to see your results. You can redirect the output to the printer.

Exercise 4: Changing the Volume Label

In this exercise, you display and modify the volume label without using the FORMAT command. Make sure that Drive A: contains the SYS DISK 6.2 disk before continuing. Follow these steps:

1. At the DOS prompt, type **vol a:** and press **Enter**. Does your disk in Drive A: contain a volume label?

2. At times, files on floppy disks change (whether the files are temporary backups or projects files); the volume label also may need to change. Change the current volume label to **DOS BOOT 6.2**.

3. You can verify a volume label in three ways. Can you list at least two? ***Hint:** The VOL command is one way.*

Exercise 5: Using the CHKDSK Command

The CHKDSK command provides information about a disk. In this exercise, you use the CHKDSK command to determine the total disk capacity of a floppy disk and a hard disk, if you have one. Follow these steps:

1. Execute CHKDSK for Drive A:. How many hidden files are on the disk? How much disk space is available? How much disk space is left? Print a hard copy of what is displayed.

2. If you have a hard disk, execute CHKDSK on Drive C:. How many 5 1/4-inch, 1.2M floppy disks would be needed to transfer *all*

files to disks? *Hint:* Look at total number of user files. Print a hard copy of what is displayed.

Continuing Problems

Refer to the complete description of the case studies in Chapter 3.

Case Study 1: Burke's Musical Instruments

Pam Oropeza's computer system has a 120M hard drive, a 5 1/4-inch high-density drive, and a 3 1/2-inch high-density drive. She has a blank 3 1/2-inch disk on which to copy some files. When she prepares to format the disk, however, she notices that the disk has no label or any writing to indicate its capacity. How can she determine whether the disk is high-density or double-density?

Case Study 2: Medical Offices of Colby, Odenthal, Bravo & Kim

For the past few days, Dr. Patricia Bravo has been working on a long medical report for a patient and found some minor errors that must be fixed. She started her favorite word processing program and opened the 60-page report file. The errors are on page 55. After page 54, the remaining text is garbage. The document is readable to page 54, but the last 6 pages contain funny characters that have no meaning. What could have happened? Is there anything that she can do? *Hint:* Data may be able to be recovered in three ways, depending on certain actions that might have been performed (such as making backups).

Case Study 3: The DOS Reference Card

In this case study, you continue creating the DOS reference card you began in Chapter 3. Several terms and DOS commands are introduced in this chapter and should be added to the reference card. Fill in the command, term, or key sequence that matches each description.

Description	Command/Term/Sequence	Type
Prepares a disk for use.	_____	Command
A partitioned section of a hard disk that DOS views as an additional hard disk.	_____	Term
Creates or modifies a name that identifies a particular disk.	_____	Command
Transfers the DOS system to a previously formatted disk.	_____	Command
Analyzes a disk, detects boot sector errors and defective clusters, including problems in DoubleSpace volumes.	_____	Command
Analyzes a disk, repairs problems in the FAT, and provides a screen report of its findings.	_____	Command

7

Challenge Problems

1. Could Ivan Dasilva format a disk for a system disk in Drive B: and reboot the computer to boot from this "new" bootable disk?

    a. What would happen if he accidentally formatted a double-density disk as a high-density disk?

    b. Is this disk usable if he reformats it for the correct capacity?

2. Joanna Alo tried to save a file, but an error message informed her that the hard disk did not have enough disk space. She cannot exit the current program to delete old files, or she may lose what she has done. What can she do?

3. Tamra Russell figured out how to save her data and decided

that it was time to clean up her hard disk. She deleted unnecessary files and removed other programs that she no longer uses. Because she removed some files, she performed CHKDSK on her hard disk. A message appeared stating that errors were found. She then used the /F switch to convert the lost chains to files.

    a. What do these files contain?

    b. What should she do with these files?

    c. Will these files affect other files or programs?

Answers to Odd-Numbered Questions

Key Term Matching Questions

1.	q	11.	k
3.	e	13.	b
5.	m	15.	o
7.	c	17.	t
9.	n	19.	p

Multiple-Choice Questions

1.	b	7.	a
3.	d	9.	b
5.	d		

True/False Questions

1.	F	7.	T
3.	F	9.	T
5.	F		

Working with Files

Chapter Summary

Chapter 8 is the first of two chapters devoted to managing your files. It explains how to examine directory listings, view the contents of files, and use the Interlnk program to transfer files between a laptop and your desktop computer. In this chapter, the following key points are presented:

- The end-of-file character ^z marks the end of ASCII files.

- The TYPE command displays an ASCII file's contents.

- You can use the DIR command with the /S switch to search an entire disk or any branch of subdirectories for files.

- The display produced by DIR lists information about file attributes, sizes, and so on. You can use the DIR command's switches and parameters to sort file names, including hidden files, and to customize the functionality of DIR.

- Interlnk provides a method to connect two computers. One computer acts as the server, and the other client computer controls both machines. Interlnk is useful for copying files to and from notebook computers. Interlnk also enables you to use the server's printer as if it were attached to the client.

Chapter Outline

   I. Using DOS to Work with Files

  II. Listing Files with DIR

      A. Issuing the DIR Command
      B. Understanding the Operation of DIR
      C. Displaying a Screen of Information with DIR
      D. Searching for Files with the DIR Command
      E. Customizing the DIR Command

 III. Viewing Files

      A. Understanding Types of Files
      B. Using the TYPE Command to View Files

  IV. Searching for Text with FIND

   V. Using Interlnk to Share Another Computer's Resources

      A. Setting Up Interlnk
      B. Loading INTERLNK.EXE
      C. Loading the Server
      D. Establishing the Interlnk Connection
      E. Using Interlnk to Transfer Files
      F. Using a Remote Printer
      G. Installing Interlnk Remotely
      H. Running Programs Remotely

Active Learning

Key Term Matching

Match the following key terms with the definitions listed after them.

____ 1. DIR /C

____ 2. TYPE

____ 3. Ctrl-C (^c)

____ 4. DIR /AR

____ 5. Binary

____ 6. |

____ 7. INTERLNK

____ 8. DIR /AA

____ 9. MORE

____ 10. ASCII

____ 11. DEBUG

____ 12. Ctrl-Z (^z)

____ 13. DIR/A-H

____ 14. EDIT

____ 15. AUTOEXEC.BAT

____ 16. >

____ 17. Ctrl-S (^s)

____ 18. DIR /S

____ 19. INTERSVR

____ 20. TSR

Definitions

a. This command displays only files that do not have the hidden attribute.

b. Programs are stored in this format.

c. A type of program that remains in memory after it is loaded.

d. This command can be used to display a text file one screen at a time.

e. A command that lists the contents of subdirectories.

f. This command is used to view the contents of a text file.

g. The DOS end-of-file character.

h. The executable program run on a computer to make it a client when linking two computers together.

i. This command displays only files that have the read-only attribute.

j. This parameter pauses the TYPE command's output.

k. This command is used to display or change the contents of a text file.

l. The character for the DOS pipe command.

m. This command displays file compression ratio.

n. The executable file run on a computer designated as a *server*, or passive slave, of another computer.

o. Text files are stored in this format.

p. The character for the DOS redirect command.

q. This command terminates the TYPE command's output.

r. This command can be used to view and edit binary files.

s. This command displays only files that have the archive attribute.

t. If you include the command SET DIRCMD=/ON/P in this file, DOS automatically executes as if you had typed DIR /P.

Multiple-Choice Questions

_____ 1. The most-frequently used DOS command is:

      a. VOL
      b. VER
      c. DIR
      d. EDIT
      e. TYPE

_____ 2. An example of an external DOS command is:

      a. DIR
      b. TYPE
      c. COPY
      d. MORE
      e. TSR

____ 3. The switch used with the DIR command to cause DOS to pause the scrolling of the screen at the end of each screen of information is:

    a. /P
    b. /S
    c. /C
    d. /A
    e. /W

____ 4. The output of the TYPE command can be paused by typing:

    a. ^C
    b. ^Z
    c. ^P
    d. ^B
    e. ^S

____ 5. Programs are stored in ____ format.

    a. graphical
    b. binary
    c. ASCII
    d. command
    e. type

8

True/False Questions

____ 1. Unless you use the /O switch with the DIR command, files and directories are listed in unsorted order.

____ 2. DOS will sort all files in descending order unless you precede your sort codes with a minus sign.

____ 3. Entering the command TYPE *.TXT displays the contents of all files ending with the TXT file extension.

____ 4. DOS allocates at least one cluster to store any file, no matter how small.

____ 5. The > symbol is known as the DOS pipe character, which instructs DOS to send a command's output to the filter that follows the pipe character.

Directed Exercises

Exercise 1: Practicing the DIR Command

This exercise gives you an opportunity to review the variations on the DIR command. Write the proper switch to use with the DIR command for the following effects, and then practice using each on your computer in the C:\DOS directory by typing **cd \dos** after your computer is booted. Make a note of the similarities and differences between each variation.

1. Display only the file names in columns across the screen.

2. List the file names only, one per line.

3. Display file compression ratio.

4. List all file names in lowercase.

5. Display only files that have the archive attribute.

6. Display only files that do not have the archive attribute.

7. List files chronologically by date and time.

8. List files in reverse alphabetical order by file extension.

Exercise 2: Using the TYPE Command

In this exercise, you practice viewing files with the TYPE command and comparing the results of this command with an ASCII format file and a binary file. This exercise assumes that your hard disk has AUTOEXEC.BAT and CONFIG.SYS files in the root directory of Drive C:.

1. After the computer is booted, make sure that you are in the root directory by typing **cd** and pressing **Enter**.

2. Verify that your hard disk has an AUTOEXEC.BAT file and a CONFIG.SYS file by entering the **dir** command. If they are not present, ask your instructor for assistance before attempting to complete the rest of this exercise.

3. Enter the command **type autoexec.bat** and view the contents on-screen.

4. Redirect the TYPE command results to a printer by entering the following:

   type autoexec.bat >prn

   Note: Be sure that you have a printer attached to your computer and turned on before attempting this step.

5. Enter the command **type config.sys** and compare the results to what you received in step 3 above. Print the contents as you did in step 4.

6. To see what would happen if you attempt to use the TYPE command on a binary file, enter the following:

   type command.com

   You should receive a few beeps and some gibberish on-screen.

Answers to Odd-Numbered Questions

8

Key Term Matching Questions

1. m	11. r
3. q	13. a
5. b	15. t
7. h	17. j
9. d	19. n

Multiple-Choice Questions

1. c
3. a
5. b

True/False Questions

1. T
3. F
5. F

Managing Your Files

Chapter Summary

Chapter 9 is the second of two chapters covering file management. This chapter explains the file-level DOS commands and offers an in-depth view of the file-level commands, concentrating on those commands used to perform housekeeping functions. This chapter covers the following main points:

- The COPY command makes copies of files on other drives, or in other directories.

- The COPY command can be used to give new names to files as they're being copied. Groups of files can be copied at one time by using wildcards in the command line.

- The MOVE command copies a file to a new location, and then deletes the original file. You can also use the MOVE command to rename directories.

- The REN or RENAME command can be used to give files another name. Each name must be unique. Groups of files can be renamed using wildcards.

- The XCOPY command copies files and directory structures. You can use the XCOPY command to duplicate floppy disks when the disks have different capacities.

- The DISKCOPY command makes exact duplicates of floppy disks. Both disks must have the same capacity.

- The FC and DISKCOMP commands compare files and floppy disks to make sure that good copies have been made. FC compares individual files or groups of individual files. DISKCOMP compares one floppy disk against another for accuracy.

- The DEL or ERASE command is used to "delete" files no longer needed. Files are not actually erased until DOS uses the directory entry or disk space for another file.

Chapter Outline

I. Copying Files

    A. Using the COPY Command
    B. Copying Groups of Files
    C. Combining Text Files
    D. Renaming Files with COPY
    E. Copying from a Device to a File

II. Using the MOVE Command

    A. Moving Directories and Files
    B. Renaming Directories with MOVE

III. Renaming Files

IV. Combining Copying and Directory Management with XCOPY

    A. Understanding the Operation of XCOPY
    B. Using XCOPY Effectively
    C. Disk Duplication with XCOPY
    D. Duplicating a Directory Branch

V. Setting Defaults for COPY, MOVE, and XCOPY

VI. Comparing Files with FC

    A. Understanding the Operation of FC
    B. Using FC to Compare a Copied File to Its Original
    C. Comparing Two Text Files

VII. Copying Entire Disks with DISKCOPY

VIII. Comparing Disks with DISKCOMP

IX. Deleting Files

    A. Understanding the Delete Operation
    B. Deleting Files from the Command Line
    C. Deleting Unwanted Files

Active Learning

Key Term Matching

Match the following key terms with the definitions listed after them.

____ 1. FC /B

____ 2. XCOPY /S

____ 3. Directories

____ 4. FC /N

____ 5. DISKCOPY

____ 6. XCOPY /A

____ 7. Internal command

____ 8. Floppy disk

____ 9. XCOPY /M

____10. FC /C

____11. SourceExpression

____12. CON

____13. DEL

____14. DISKCOMP

____15. TargetExpression

____16. MOVE

____17. REN

____18. External command

____19. Wildcard

____20. COPY

Definitions

a. This command can be used to change the name of a file.

b. A command that copies a group of files and removes the archive bit from them.

c. A DOS utility command that is included in COMMAND.COM.

d. This command creates a copy of files on other drives or in other directories.

e. A command used to compare individual files or groups of individual files with the parameter to perform a binary comparison showing the hexadecimal address and value of every differing byte.

f. This command is used to compare one floppy disk against another for accuracy.

g. A character such as **?** or ***** that can replace one or more characters in a file name.

9

h. This command removes files that are no longer needed; they are not actually erased until DOS uses the directory entry or disk space for another file.

i. A flexible plastic platter encased in an envelope that can store files when it is inserted into and subsequently removed from a disk drive.

j. The combination of drive, path, and file name parameters that specifies the location of a file or disk from which you are attempting to copy.

k. A command that copies the files found in any directories that branch off from the source directory, ignoring empty directories.

l. A DOS utility command that must be executed by typing the file name.

m. A command used to compare individual files or groups of individual files with the parameter to ignore the case of alphabetic characters when making the comparison.

n. These cannot be removed with the ERASE command.

o. This command creates a duplicate of a file in a new location, then deletes the original file.

p. The device name for console, a device constructed using your keyboard and monitor.

q. A command used to compare individual files or groups of individual files with the parameter to include the line numbers of lines reported in the output.

r. The combination of drive, path, and file name parameters used to specify the destination of a command.

s. Used to make an exact duplicate of a floppy disk onto one that has the same capacity.

t. A command that copies only files with the archive attribute set without modifying the file's attributes.

Multiple-Choice Questions

____ 1. The DOS command that can be used to copy both files and directory structures to duplicate floppy disks when the disks have different capacities is:

      a. FC
      b. COPY
      c. DISKCOPY
      d. XCOPY
      e. FCOPY

____ 2. The ____ wildcard can be used with the COPY command to replace several characters in the file name.

      a. ^
      b. %
      c. #
      d. ?
      e. *

____ 3. The command used to make exact duplicates of floppy disks of the same capacity is:

      a. COPY
      b. DISKCOPY
      c. DISKCOMP
      d. XCOPY
      e. FC

____ 4. Which of the following source-file parameters would not be a valid choice to use with the COPY command?

      a. B:
      b. FILE1+FILE2
      c. b:*.*\DOS
      d. a:\DOS\FILE3.TXT
      e. FILE4.*

____ 5. Which parameter when used with the MOVE command indicates to overwrite files with the same name without prompting?

      a. /Y
      b. /-Y
      c. /P
      d. /-P
      e. /A

_____ 6. The DOS command that can be used to rename directories is:

    a. REN
    b. MOVE
    c. RD
    d. RENDIR
    e. FC

_____ 7. Which parameter causes XCOPY to remove the archive bit from any files copied?

    a. /A
    b. /D
    c. /M
    d. /E
    e. /S

_____ 8. The _____ command is used to compare individual files or groups of individual files.

    a. FC
    b. DISKCOMP
    c. COMPARE
    d. COPY
    e. REN

_____ 9. Which of the following is an internal command?

    a. DISKCOPY
    b. FC
    c. DISKCOMP
    d. COPY
    e. XCOPY

_____10. Which command can copy hidden source files?

    a. XCOPY
    b. COPY
    c. COPY /A
    d. XCOPY /H
    e. DISKCOPY

True/False Questions

____ 1. If COPY detects an attempt to copy a single source file to itself, the copy operation is aborted.

____ 2. If the source and target parameters used with the MOVE command represent the same file, DOS prompts you before erasing the source file.

____ 3. The REN command may change the name of the directory, but its physical location on the disk remains unchanged.

____ 4. You can use the /Y switch with the COPY command to indicate that you don't want to be prompted when about to overwrite files with the same name.

____ 5. Using the /P parameter with the XCOPY command, you can specify a group of files with a wildcard and then decide which files you actually want to copy when XCOPY prompts you.

____ 6. Using the COPY command is much easier to use than the XCOPY command.

____ 7. All files created by XCOPY have the archive attribute set automatically, even if the original source file does not have the archive attribute.

____ 8. While the FC command is used to compare files, the DISKCOMP command is used to compare one hard disk to another.

____ 9. If you don't provide a drive or path, DOS uses the current drive or path for the destination with COPY or XCOPY.

____10. Although the DEL command does not remove directories, you can use it to erase hidden or system files.

9

▶ Directed Exercises

Exercise 1: Using COPY and XCOPY

In this exercise, you compare the differences between the internal COPY command and the external XCOPY command. This exercise requires that you use a computer system with a hard drive.

1. With the DOS prompt displaying Drive C: as the current drive, create a temporary directory called DOSTEST. Change to the DOSTEST directory.

2. Using the COPY command, copy *.COM files from the DOS directory to the DOSTEST directory. Keep track of how long it takes from the time you press Enter to when the DOS prompt tells you that the copy function is complete.

3. Using the XCOPY command, perform the same copy function as before. Again, keep track of how long it takes. Which DOS command performed the copy function the fastest? Why do you think one is faster than the other? Make sure that the printer is connected and turned on, then print a directory listing of the DOSTEST directory to the printer (**DIR > PRN**).

4. For this part of the exercise, you need a blank formatted floppy disk. Create a new subdirectory under DOSTEST called NEWSUB.

5. Copy ***.*** from DOSTEST to NEWSUB. Your current working directory should be DOSTEST. Make sure that the floppy disk is in the disk drive.

6. Use XCOPY with the /S switch to copy all the files, including the NEWSUB directory, to the floppy disk. Explain how you could use the COPY command to perform the same function.

7. The XCOPY command provides many enhancements over the COPY command. One enhancement is the capability to copy files by date. This enhancement enables you to copy files on or after a specified date. Using the /D switch with the XCOPY command, copy all files with a COM extension and a date of 9-27-93 from the DOS directory to the DOSTEST directory. How many files were listed? Make sure that the printer is on, then print a directory listing of the DOSTEST directory to the printer (**DIR> PRN**).

8. Create another subdirectory under the DOSTEST directory called EMPTYSUB. Do not copy any files into this directory. Using the same floppy disk from before and the XCOPY command with the /S and /E switches, copy all files from the DOSTEST directory to the floppy disk.

9. At the DOS command line, execute the DIR command using the /S switch, and send the output to a file called DIR_HD.LOG.

10. Execute the same DIR command, but on the floppy disk, and redirect the output to DIR_FLOP.LOG. Print the file DIR_FLOP.LOG to the printer.

Exercise 2: Practicing COPY CON and Combining Files

This exercise demonstrates how to use the COPY CON command from the DOS command line to create files and how to use the COPY command to combine the contents of two or more files into a single file. Follow these steps:

1. At the DOS command line, type **copy con sample.txt** and press **Enter**. Notice that the DOS prompt does not appear at the beginning of the second line because you are "inside" a file. Type **This is a sample file that contains 1 line of text.** and press **Enter** again. On the third line, type **^z** (Ctrl-Z) to return to the DOS prompt.

2. Create a second file by typing **copy con sample2.txt** and pressing **Enter**. On the second line, type **This is another sample file.** and press **Enter** again. End the file by typing **^z** (Ctrl-Z) just as you did in step 1.

3. Using the COPY command, combine the two files you just created to create a third file called EXPERIMT.TXT by typing the following:

       copy sample.txt + sample2.txt experimt.txt

   The contents of EXPERIMT.TXT should look like the following:

   ```
   This is a sample file that contains 1 line of text.

   This is another sample file.
   ```

4. Direct the contents of EXPERIMT.TXT to the printer.

5. Now use the COPY command to combine all files ending with the file extension TXT to SAMPLE.TXT. Was a DOS error message displayed, indicating that you were about to copy over an already existing file? Did the contents of SAMPLE.TXT change when you executed the COPY statement, or are the contents the same as when you first started this exercise? Are EXPERIMT.TXT and SAMPLE.TXT the same file size? Are the contents of the two files the same?

9

6. Type **copy *.* new_file.txt** and press **Enter**. What is the result of performing this command?

Exercise 3: Renaming Files

This exercise demonstrates the use of the REN command from the DOS command line and the Rename command from within the DOS Shell. Follow these steps:

1. At the DOS command line, rename the file EXPERIMT.TXT to EXPERIMT.DAT. Does the REN command create a duplicate of the source file? Provide an example of why you would use the REN command.

2. Rename EXPERIMT.DAT to EXPERIMT.NEW. Type **dir** and press **Enter**. Print a hard copy of the screen display.

3. Use the DOS wildcard to rename all files ending with the file extension TXT to the new file extension NEW. What precautions should you take when using wildcards with the REN command?

4. From the DOS Shell, select the file EXPERIMT.NEW and rename this file to EXPERIMT.TXT. How does this activity compare to using the REN command? Make a note of similarities and differences. Which method do you prefer?

Exercise 4: Duplicating Entire Disks

This exercise requires that you have a bootable floppy disk (that is, one with the operating system's hidden files) and a second floppy disk of the same size (the second disk does not have to be formatted). Follow these steps:

1. Use the CHKDSK command to be sure that the bootable disk has the operating system's hidden files.

2. Create a subdirectory on the bootable disk named **TESTSUB** and copy several files into it from your computer's hard disk.

3. Create a second subdirectory called **TESTSUB2** inside the TESTSUB directory, and copy several files into it as well.

4. Make a subdirectory on your hard drive called **XCOPYTST** and copy the entire contents of your bootable floppy to that subdirectory using the XCOPY command with the /S parameter. Did the operating system's hidden files get copied to the hard drive? How would you find out?

5. Now use the DISKCOPY command to make an exact duplicate of the bootable floppy disk. Did the operating system's hidden files get copied this time?

Exercise 5: Comparing Entire Disks and Individual Files

In this exercise, you practice comparing entire disks and individual files. This exercise assumes that you have completed exercise 4. Follow these steps:

1. Enter the DISKCOMP command with no drive parameters to compare the two floppy disks prepared in exercise 4. Are they exactly the same?

2. Now enter the DISKCOMP command with no drive parameters to compare one of the disks with any other disk that is *not* the same. How do the results of this action compare to the results of the previous step?

3. Use the FC command to compare the contents of the COMMAND.COM file on your floppy disk to the COMMAND.COM on the hard disk by using the parameter to perform a binary comparison, showing the hexadecimal address and value of every differing byte. Were they the same?

4. Now use the FC command to compare all of the files in the TESTSUB directory of the floppy disk to the files in the TESTSUB directory on the hard disk. Are they exact?

5. Use the FC command with the /N parameter to compare the contents of the **FCTEST1** and **FCTEST2** files on the data file diskette under the **\ch9** directory. How do the results from this command differ from the last FC commands entered?

9

Continuing Problems

Refer to the complete description of the case studies in Chapter 3.

Case Study 1: Burke's Musical Instruments

Debbie Burke asked Issa Freeman to make backup copies of the data on the computer's hard disk onto floppy disks that can be stored at another location in case of fire. Issa isn't exactly sure how to do it. He is familiar with the COPY command but thinks it will take too much time to copy all the files in the hard drive one by one. Which command(s) should he use to create the backup copies?

Case Study 2: Medical Offices of Colby, Odenthal, Bravo & Kim

Dr. Lisa Odenthal's assistant, Javier Mendoza, made copies of some important floppy disks for her. After some changes were made to a couple of files, he made a second set of backup disks. Now Dr. Odenthal has two sets of backup disks and isn't sure which one matches the current files. Is there an easy way for her to find out which backup disk matches the most current files?

Case Study 3: The DOS Reference Card

In this case study, you continue creating the DOS reference card you began in Chapter 3. Several terms and DOS commands are introduced in this chapter and should be added to the reference card. Fill in the command, term, or key sequence that matches each description.

Description	Command/Term/Sequence	Type
A file containing only standard ASCII characters.		Term
Changes the name of a file.		Command
Sets the computer to check the accuracy of data written or copied to a disk.		Command

Description	Command/Term/Sequence	Type
Marks the end of an ASCII file.	_____	Term
Removes a file from a directory.	_____	Command
Copies files between disk drives and/or devices, either keeping or changing the name.	_____	Command
Displays from the designated files all the lines that match (or do not match) the specified string.	_____	Command
Replaces files on one disk with files of the same name from another disk; adds files to a disk by copying them from another disk.	_____	Command

 # Challenge Problems

1. Eric Yu has been working on a proposal all day, creating multiple documents that use graphic images. In order to keep track of where all the necessary pieces are for this proposal, he created a handful of subdirectories to act as separators. This scheme works well, but he wants to create a duplicate of his tree structure on another disk. He could create each directory separately and copy each file into the appropriate directory, but this task would be very time-consuming. Is there an easier way to create a mirror copy of your tree structure without having to spend so much time?

2. How could Tony Gawel combine 30 separate files (FILE0001.TXT through FILE0030.TXT) into one large file called COMBO.TXT while using the COPY command on the DOS command line? One problem is the fact that only 127 characters can be typed on the DOS command line at any one time. *Hint:* There is more than one possible answer.

9

3. When working on a project, such as writing a computer program, programmer Marvyn Lindsey makes copies of his work on separate disks. When he is writing program code for an application, the files can be numerous, and some can get rather large. Often, all the program code files will not fit on a single floppy disk; instead, they must be stored on many floppy disks. Using the COPY command would be tedious and time-consuming. What DOS command can Marvyn use with wildcards to duplicate files as well as directories over many floppy disks?

Answers to Odd-Numbered Questions

Key Term Matching Questions

1.	e	11.	j
3.	n	13.	h
5.	s	15.	r
7.	c	17.	a
9.	b	19.	g

Multiple-Choice Questions

1.	d	7.	c
3.	b	9.	d
5.	a		

True/False Questions

1.	T	7.	T
3.	F	9.	T
5.	T		

Data Files to Active Learning

Exercise	Beginning Name	Ending Name
Directed Exercise		
1	DOSTEST directory NEWSUB directory EMPTYSUB directory DIR_HD.LOG DIR_FLOP.LOG	DOSTEST directory NEWSUB directory EMPTYSUB directory DIR_HD.LOG DIR_FLOP.LOG
2	SAMPLE.TXT SAMPLE2.TXT EXPERIMT.TXT NEW_FILE.TXT	SAMPLE.TXT SAMPLE2.TXT EXPERIMT.TXT NEW_FILE.TXT
3	EXPERIMT.TXT SAMPLE.TXT SAMPLE2.TXT NEW_FILE.TXT	EXPERIMT.NEW SAMPLE.NEW SAMPLE2.NEW NEW_FILE.NEW
4	TESTSUB directory TESTSUB2 directory XCOPYTST directory	TESTSUB directory TESTSUB2 directory XCOPYTST directory
5	FCTEST1 FCTEST2	FCTEST1 FCTEST2

9

Protecting Your Data

Chapter Summary

Chapter 10 covers the important issues involved in safeguarding the most important part of the computer system: the computer data. This chapter explains how to protect your computer files from various menaces such as static electricity, excessive heat, and erratic electrical power. It presents common-sense solutions to data protection, as well as how to use the backup programs supplied with MS-DOS. Chapter 10 also includes a discussion of computer viruses and explains how to use the Microsoft Anti-Virus program to stop them.

Chapter 10 covers the following key points:

- You can protect your computer hardware equipment by following common-sense safety precautions.

- The MSBACKUP command produces special copies of your program and data-file backup sets. Backup sets normally are used for recovering lost data.

- The RESTORE command reads files from backup sets and restores the files to their original directories on another disk.

- You can protect yourself from data loss by faithfully following a backup policy.

- Viruses can damage your system, but you can use the Microsoft Anti-Virus program to protect your data.

- You can best protect your data from computer viruses by purchasing only tested software and using MSAV or Microsoft Anti-Virus for Windows to check all new software and all floppy disks.

Chapter Outline

I. Avoiding Data Loss

    A. Preventing Software Failures
    B. Preventing Mistakes

II. Understanding Microsoft Backup

    A. Configuring the Backup Programs
    B. Understanding Microsoft Backup Functions
    C. Setting Up a Backup Policy
    D. Issuing the MSBACKUP Command

III. Using Microsoft Backup

    A. Performing a Full Backup
    B. Performing Intermediate Backups
    C. Special-Purpose Backups
    D. Using Other Backup Options
    E. Restoring Backup Files

IV. Understanding Computer Viruses

    A. Understanding How Viruses Spread
    B. Fighting Viruses with Microsoft Anti-Virus
    C. Using the Windows Version of Microsoft Anti-Virus
    D. Guarding Against Infection

Active Learning

Key Term Matching

Match the following key terms with the definitions listed after them.

_____ 1. Compression   _____ 11. DMA Buffer

_____ 2. MSAV   _____ 12. Static electricity

_____ 3. Data loss   _____ 13. CHKLIST.MS

_____ 4. Bugs   _____ 14. File fragmentation

_____ 5. Computer viruses   _____ 15. MWAV

_____ 6. Overheating   _____ 16. Full backup

_____ 7. Incremental backup   _____ 17. DEFAULT.SET

_____ 8. Copy-protected   _____ 18. Differential backup

_____ 9. Clean   _____ 19. Archive attribute

_____ 10. ATTRIB   _____ 20. Detect

Definitions

a. Flawed instructions present in a minority of software packages.

b. Copies every file on your hard disk so that you can re-create your system if your hard disk is destroyed.

c. The option of Microsoft Anti-Virus that looks for viruses and tells you what it finds, but does not destroy the viruses.

d. Place a "touch pad" on your desk to avoid problems from this.

e. If files on your hard disk have this feature when you do a backup, they might not restore properly to a destination disk.

f. A method of backing up files, causing fewer disks and requiring less time to complete a backup.

g. This method copies only files that are new or have been changed since the last full backup, reusing the same floppy disks for each backup.

10

h. A command that can be used to "turn on" the archive attribute.

i. Your computer might perform erratically when this happens; it may even jumble data.

j. The Microsoft Anti-Virus program included with DOS 6.2 to run from the command line.

k. If the size of this is too small, you will not be able to perform a backup until it is increased.

l. When pieces of files are scattered around a hard disk instead of being in contiguous space.

m. The name of the file provided with DOS that can be used as the setup file used for backup.

n. This method copies only new files or files that have been changed since the last full backup was performed but requires an additional set of disks each time.

o. This can be prevented by keeping current backups of your hard disk and any floppy disks that contain important data, and by scanning for viruses.

p. The option of Microsoft Anti-Virus that destroys computer viruses.

q. A file created in every directory by Microsoft Anti-Virus containing identifying information about the files in that directory to help it detect any virus infections that have occurred since the file was created.

r. An attribute that indicates a file needs to be backed up.

s. The anti-virus program included with DOS to run in a Windows environment.

t. A purposely-destructive program that can alter or destroy your files, programs, and/or file allocation table.

Multiple-Choice Questions

____ 1. Which of the following is not a standard recommendation to avoid damaged disks?

     a. Store disks in a safe place.
     b. Avoid spilling liquids on disks.
     c. Do not place diskettes on top of televisions or microwave ovens.
     d. Do not use protective covers.
     e. Do not use a ballpoint pen to write on disk labels.

____ 2. Which backup method copies every file on your hard disk?

     a. differential backup
     b. incremental backup
     c. full backup
     d. catalog backup
     e. distributed backup

____ 3. Which of the following statements is true about restoring files?

     a. You must use the RESTORE command to restore files backed up with MSBACKUP.
     b. You must use the MSRESTORE command to restore files backed up with MSBACKUP.
     c. The restore operation has an option to format the destination disk.
     d. Files restored from a full backup set to a freshly formatted disk are not fragmented.
     e. Restoring files from a full backup set might result in fragmented destination files if the source files were fragmented when they were backed up.

____ 4. Which of the following options for Microsoft Anti-Virus results in the destruction of any viruses that are found?

     a. Detect
     b. Configure
     c. Detect & Clean
     d. CHKLIST
     e. Report

10

_____ 5. Hardware problems can generally be caused by all of the following except

    a. static electricity.
    b. overheating.
    c. clogged or blocked air vents on the computer.
    d. erratic power fluctuations.
    e. computer viruses.

_____ 6. The file attribute that triggers the backup program to make a copy of that file is:

    a. Archive
    b. Copy
    c. Backup
    d. System
    e. There is no such attribute.

_____ 7. MSBACKUP allows you to do all of the following except

    a. copy files from a hard disk to a floppy disk.
    b. copy files from a floppy disk to a hard disk.
    c. compare files on your backup copies with the originals.
    d. restore the copied files to another disk of your choice.
    e. All of these answers can be done with MSBACKUP.

_____ 8. The name of the file that stores the default setup selections for MWBACKUP is:

    a. MWBACKUP.INI
    b. SETUP.FIL
    c. DEFAULT.SET
    d. DEFAULT.INI
    e. BACKUP.SET

_____ 9. Which of the following is not a basic function represented by an icon in the Windows backup program MWBACKUP?

    a. Compare
    b. Restore
    c. Configure
    d. Exit
    e. Backup

_____ 10. Which of the following statements is not true about computer viruses?

    a. Uploading software to bulletin boards can infect your computer.

    b. Many viruses are spread when a computer boots from a floppy disk that carries the virus.

    c. Downloading software from bulletin boards increases your chances of encountering a virus.

    d. You can get a virus from loading and running an infected program on the computer.

    e. Your best defense against viruses is a virus-scanning program.

True/False Questions

_____ 1. Using a ballpoint pen to write on flexible disk labels could result in a damaged disk.

_____ 2. Files copied to a backup disk with the MSBACKUP program have the same format as files on your hard disk or files copied with the XCOPY command.

_____ 3. If you do not now use Microsoft Windows but add that operating environment to your system later, you must reinstall DOS to install the Windows version of the backup program.

_____ 4. A computer virus often does its damage by altering the disk's file allocation table (FAT) and marking clusters as bad or unavailable.

_____ 5. Although an incremental backup must start on a new target disk, a differential backup gives you the option of adding backup files to disks that have been used as part of a set.

_____ 6. Even if your computer passes the compatibility test for doing backups, if your DMA buffer size is too small, you will not be able to perform a backup, compare, or restore files until the DMA buffer size is increased.

_____ 7. When you use the /R switch with MSAV, it creates a file called CHKLIST.MS which lists the number of files MSAV scanned, the number of viruses detected, and the number of viruses removed.

10

____ 8. You should use air-conditioning in a computer room during the summer because you might get jumbled data if your computer gets overheated.

____ 9. The MSBACKUP program can be used to restore copies on your backup floppy disks to the hard disk, in either their original location or a new location, or to another floppy disk in usable form.

____10. Backup programs can spread a single file across more than one floppy disk or show only one file per disk that actually contains the data that originally appeared in many files on your hard disk.

▶ Directed Exercises

Exercise 1: Using MSBACKUP from the DOS Prompt

In this exercise, you practice using the MSBACKUP command from the DOS prompt. This exercise assumes that you are using a computer with a hard disk and that you have completed the exercises in Chapter 9. You also need a floppy disk for this exercise. Use the same disk that you used in Chapter 9, exercise 1.

1. Back up all the files and subdirectories for DOSTEST by using the MSBACKUP command from the DOS prompt. If this is the first time that MSBACKUP has been run from this machine, the compatibility test will automatically run before you are able to proceed with the backup.

2. After the MSBACKUP command executes, use the Compare option to verify that the copies are accurate.

3. When you return to the DOS prompt, perform a directory listing of the backup disk and redirect the output to the printer. How many files are listed? What does each file listed represent?

4. How can you estimate the number of floppy disks you need to back up all of Drive C:? *Hint:* Use the CHKDSK command. Estimate the number of floppy disks you would need to back up only your data files. Redirect the output from the CHKDSK command to the printer (**CHKDSK > PRN**).

5. Remove the DOSTEST directory and all its subdirectories and files. Verify that these directories and files are gone by using the DIR command.

6. Using the backup disk, restore the DOSTEST directory and its files and subdirectories.

7. One important factor often overlooked when backing up data is the labeling of the backup disks. Design a label that provides the backup date and time, the path backed up, the disk number, and the total number of disks in the backup set. Why is tracking the date and time of a backup important?

Exercise 2: Developing a Backup Policy

Interview a computer support manager or another person who has the responsibility for preventing data loss and determine what the backup policy for the company is and how it was developed. Write a backup policy for your own data and explain how it might differ from a backup policy at a large company where there might be thousands of files.

Exercise 3: Using Microsoft Backup for Windows

In this exercise, you practice using the MWBACKUP command for Windows. This exercise assumes that you are using a computer with a hard disk that has Microsoft Windows installed and that you have completed the exercises in Chapter 9. You also need a floppy disk for this exercise. Use the same disk that you used in Chapter 9, exercise 1.

1. Start the MWBACKUP command from Microsoft Windows by clicking on the **File Run** option in Program Manager and typing **MWBACKUP**.

2. When the program executes, click on the Backup icon and make a backup copy of all the files and subdirectories for DOSTEST onto your floppy disk.

3. Use the Compare option to verify that the copies are accurate.

4. Go to the Windows File Manager by pressing **Alt-Esc**, and then click on the File Manager icon.

10

5. Remove the DOSTEST directory and all its subdirectories and files from the hard disk. Verify that these directories and files are gone.

6. Using the backup disk, restore the DOSTEST directory, its subdirectories, and its files.

7. Compare the results of this exercise to the results of exercise 1. Which was easier? Which did you prefer? Ask two other students in your class which method they think was easier and which they prefer.

Exercise 4: Scanning For Viruses With MSAV

In this exercise, you practice using the MSAV program to scan for computer viruses, both on your hard disk and floppy disk. Follow these steps:

1. Start the program by typing **MSAV** at the DOS prompt and pressing **Enter**.

2. When the main MSAV menu appears, select the option for Detect to begin the processing of scanning for viruses. Did you find any viruses? If the program detected any viruses, select Clean to destroy the virus and continue searching for more.

3. When the current drive has been scanned for viruses, read the report displayed on-screen.

4. Exit the program, place a floppy disk in Drive A:, and restart the program by typing the following:

      MSAV A: /R

   MSAV creates a file called MSAV.RPT in the floppy disk's root directory.

5. Print the contents of the MSAV.RPT file.

Exercise 5: Listing Viruses

This exercise increases your awareness of viruses and shows you how to find out more information about a virus that may interest you. Follow these steps:

1. Start MSAV and press **F9** to see the virus list.

2. Use the scroll bars to scan through the list of known viruses. When you find a virus about which you would like more information, click on the virus's name.

3. Search for the Christmas Boot virus by entering its name in the blue box and selecting Find Next.

4. Search for the Stoned virus in the same way.

5. Read the descriptions of five other viruses whose names appeal to you. Do you see a pattern or are they all different? What are the effects of each?

 # Continuing Problems

Refer to the complete description of the case studies in Chapter 3.

Case Study 1: Burke's Musical Instruments

Debbie Burke has decided to protect her computer's data by implementing a backup policy. She has asked Pamela Oropeza to create two full backups and develop a policy for future backups. Would they be more protected with incremental or differential backups, or should they do full backups each time?

Case Study 2: Medical Offices of Colby, Odenthal, Bravo & Kim

Dr. Patricia Bravo is very worried about data loss due to computer viruses, especially since her roommate's school has been infected and Dr. Bravo often brings computer files back and forth between home and office. How often should she check for viruses? Is there any way to automate the process?

Case Study 3: The DOS Reference Card

In this case study, you continue creating the DOS reference card you began in Chapter 3. Several terms and DOS commands are introduced in this chapter and should be added to the reference card. Fill in the command, term, or key sequence that matches each description.

Description	Command/Term/Sequence	Type
Flawed instructions in a minority of software packages.	_____	Term
Monitors your system to detect and remove computer viruses.	_____	Command
A program created for the purpose of damaging data.	_____	Term
DOS version of a program to create backups.	_____	Command
Windows version of a program to create backups.	_____	Command

 # Challenge Problems

1. Willie Ysais has been asked to make a full backup of his company's computer but isn't sure how many disks they will need. The computer has two high-density floppy drives, one 5-1/4 inch and one 3-1/2 inch, and 89MB of files. How many 5-1/4 inch floppy disks will it take to do the job? How many 3-1/2 inch floppies?

2. Pingkan Sitoares has a favorite sweater made of synthetic fabrics and whenever she wears it, she gets sparks when she touches the doorknob. What can she do to protect her computer from the static electricity generated by her favorite sweater?

Answers to Odd-Numbered Questions

Key Term Matching Questions

1. f		11. k	
3. o		13. q	
5. t		15. s	
7. n		17. m	
9. p		19. r	

Multiple-Choice Questions

1. d	7. e
3. d	9. d
5. e	

True/False Questions

1. T	7. F
3. T	9. T
5. F	

10

Emergency Procedures

Chapter Summary

Chapter 11 discusses how you can recover from catastrophic errors or events. It explains how to undelete files, unformat a drive, and recover data on the hard disk. In particular, the chapter presents the following information:

1. You can use the UNFORMAT command to undo an accidental format. The efficiency of the command is increased if your newly formatted disk has a MIRROR file available on it.

2. Deleted files can be restored to the disk by using the UNDELETE command.

3. UNDELETE offers three different methods for restoring deleted files. The delete sentry and delete tracker methods require the UNDELETE program to be loaded as a memory-resident program, whereas the standard method can be used without the overhead of a TSR program.

Chapter Outline

I. Unformatting a Disk

    A. Recovering from an Accidental Format
    B. Recovering from an Accidental Format without a MIRROR Image File
    C. Rebuilding a Partition Table

II. Recovering Deleted Files with UNDELETE

    A. Using UNDELETE from the Command Line
    B. Recovering Files with UNDELETE
    C. Using the DOS Directory to Recover a File

III. Using the Microsoft Undelete Program for Windows

    A. Configuring Microsoft Undelete
    B. Selecting Files to Recover
    C. Recovering Files
    D. Using Other Options

Active Learning

Key Term Matching

Match the following key terms with the definitions listed after them.

____ 1. UNFORMAT /U

____ 2. Root directory

____ 3. SENTRY

____ 4. FORMAT /U

____ 5. TSR

____ 6. RECOVER

____ 7. UNFORMAT /J

____ 8. File fragmentation

____ 9. MIRORSAV.FIL

____ 10. UNDELETE /DS

____ 11. FAT

____ 12. UNDELETE /DT

____ 13. Boot record

____ 14. SUBDIR.001

____ 15. UNDELETE.INI

____ 16. PARTNSAV.FIL

____ 17. MIRROR

____ 18. UNFORMAT /L

____ 19. PCTRACKER.DEL

____ 20. UNFORMAT /TEST

Definitions

a. A copy of this table is contained in the MIRROR image file.

b. If you have used this command, no MIRROR image file is created and UNFORMAT will not work.

c. The UNFORMAT command has difficulty dealing with this condition.

d. This command searches a formatted disk and lists the file and directory names found.

e. The name assigned to the first subdirectory that was recovered by UNFORMAT but without its original name also being recovered.

f. This command tells DOS to use the delete sentry method, recovering only files stored in the SENTRY directory.

g. This image file contains a copy of the disk's FAT, root directory, and boot record and saves this information in a normally unused portion of the disk.

h. Causes UNFORMAT to verify that the MIRROR image file accurately reflects the current disk information.

i. A hidden subdirectory that contains copies of deleted files.

j. A configuration file used by the UNDELETE command.

k. This command attempts to unformat a disk without the benefit of a MIRROR image file.

l. This file contains the partition table used by MIRROR to recover from a corrupted hard-disk partition table.

m. A copy of this directory's information is stored in the MIRROR image file.

n. This command instructs DOS to use the delete tracking method of recovering the specified files.

o. This hidden file contains information required by DOS to locate the MIRROR image file.

p. The damage done by this command can be reversed by the UNFORMAT command.

q. This command provides a test run to indicate whether UNFORMAT can unformat a disk successfully.

r. A type of file that remains in memory, also known as memory-resident.

s. A hidden file that records information about deleted files.

t. A copy of this record is stored in the MIRROR image file.

Multiple-Choice Questions

_____ 1. The DOS utility used to rebuild a damaged partition table on your hard disk is called

      a. UNDELETE
      b. RECOVER
      c. FORMAT
      d. UNFORMAT
      e. MIRROR

_____ 2. The FORMAT utility creates a hidden file named _____ that contains information required by DOS to locate the MIRROR image file.

      a. MIRROR.SAV
      b. MIRORSAV.FIL
      c. FORMAT.SAV
      d. MIRROR.DAT
      e. MIRORSAV.DAT

_____ 3. Which of the following information is not contained in the MIRROR image file?

      a. FAT
      b. Root directory
      c. Root-level files
      d. Boot record
      e. All of these answers are contained in the MIRROR image file.

_____ 4. The UNDELETE utility's Delete Tracker protection uses a hidden file named:

      a. PCTRACKER.DEL
      b. TRACKER.DEL
      c. DELETE.DAT
      d. UNDELETE.DAT
      e. SENTRY.DEL

_____ 5. Which of the following UNDELETE options enables delete sentry protection on the specified drives using the information found in UNDELETE.INI?

    a. /LOAD
    b. /ALL
    c. /T
    d. /DS
    e. /S

True/False Questions

_____ 1. If you use the /U switch with FORMAT, the UNFORMAT command will not work.

_____ 2. When the UNFORMAT utility finds root-level files but cannot recover their names, it assigns each a new name such as FILE0001, FILE0002, and so on.

_____ 3. If you discover that you accidentally deleted a file, immediately try to recover it because the longer you wait, the less likely the UNDELETE command will be able to work.

_____ 4. An incapacity to deal with file fragmentation severely limits the usefulness of UNFORMAT.

_____ 5. You can use the UNDELETE command to recover files and directories that have accidentally been deleted from the disk because the information has not been deleted; only the entry in the FAT has been changed.

▶ Directed Exercises

Exercise 1: Using the UNFORMAT Command on a Floppy Disk

This exercise is designed to give you practice using the UNFORMAT command. The exercise is written to be performed on a floppy disk but the effects would be the same if you were working on a hard disk. This exercise assumes that the FORMAT and UNFORMAT commands are available on Drive C:.

1. Place a floppy disk in Drive A: and format it as a data disk by typing **format a:** and pressing **Enter**.

2. When the format is complete, copy several files to the floppy disk from Drive C:.

3. Type **dir a: /ah** and press **Enter** to view a list of the disk's contents.

   a. Locate the MIRROR image file. What is its name?

   b. Make a note of how many files are on the disk and the file names.

4. Now safe-format the floppy disk by typing **format a:** and pressing **Enter**.

5. When the format is complete, enter the DIR command again to verify that the disk has been formatted.

6. Enter the UNFORMAT command with the /TEST option to indicate whether this disk can be unformatted successfully. (Type **unformat a: /test** and press **Enter**.)

   a. What was the screen's response?

   b. Did this process recover any files? (**Hint:** Use the DIR command to see.)

7. Now enter the UNFORMAT command and recover all the files by typing **unformat a:** and pressing **Enter**.

   a. What is the first instruction the UNFORMAT command gives you?

   b. Did the screen display a warning?

   c. When was the last time MIRROR was used?

Exercise 2: Using the UNDELETE Command

In this exercise, you practice using the UNDELETE command. The exercise is written to be performed on a floppy disk, but the effects would be the same if you were working on a hard disk. This exercise assumes that the UNDELETE command is available on Drive C: and that a path has been set to its directory (usually called \DOS). Use the data diskette. Type **cd \ch11** and follow these steps:

1. Type **dir a:** and press **Enter** to view a list of the disk's contents. Make a note of how many files are on the disk and the file names.

2. Now delete all files ending with the TXT extension by typing **del *.txt** and pressing **Enter**.

3. When the deletion is complete, enter the DIR command again to verify that the files are not there.

4. Enter the UNDELETE command with the /LIST option to indicate which files can be undeleted successfully. (Type **undelete a: /list** and press **Enter**.)

    a. What was the screen's response?

    b. Did this process recover any files? (***Hint:*** Use the DIR command again to see.)

5. Now enter the UNDELETE command and recover all the files by typing **undelete a: /dos** and pressing **Enter**.

    a. What is the result of the command?

    b. Did the screen display a warning or ask any questions? What were they?

6. Type **dir a:** and press **Enter** to view a list of the disk's contents. Make a note of how many files are on the disk and the file names. Does the list match the one you created in step 1?

7. Again delete all files ending with the TXT extension by typing **del *.txt** and pressing **Enter**.

8. When the deletion is complete, enter the DIR command again to verify that the files are not there.

9. Now enter the UNDELETE command with the /ALL option to recover all the files by typing **undelete a: /all** and pressing **Enter**.

    a. What is the result of the command?

    b. Did the screen display a warning or ask any questions?

    c. How does this option compare to the one used in step 5?

10. Delete all the files again and use the UNDELETE command with the /DS switch to use the delete sentry method.

   a. Did this method work?

   b. How does this compare to the previous actions?

11. Repeat the process one last time and use the UNDELETE command with the /DT switch to use the delete tracking method of recovering the specified files.

   a. Did this method work?

   b. How does this compare to the previous actions?

   c. Of all the options you tried, which method do you prefer?

Exercise 3: Using the UNDELETE Program for Windows

In this exercise, you practice using the UNDELETE program for Windows. This exercise is written to be performed on a floppy disk, but the effects would be the same if you were working on a hard disk. This exercise assumes that the UNDELETE command has been installed through Windows. Use the data diskette. Type **cd \ch11** and follow these steps:

1. Go to File Manager, then click the **Drive/Dir** button or choose Change **D**rive/Directory from the **F**ile menu to make Drive A:\CH11 the default drive. View the list of the disk's contents, and make a note of how many files are on the disk and the file names.

2. Now delete the UNDEL1.TXT file by highlighting it and pressing **Del**.

3. When the deletion is complete, click on the UNDELETE icon with the highlight on UNDEL1.TXT to indicate whether the file can be undeleted successfully.

   a. What was the screen's response?

   b. Does the line at the bottom of the screen indicate that this file can be 100 percent undeleted?

11

4. From the **File** menu, choose Undelete, and then choose Undelete **To** from the **File** menu.

   a. What is the result?

   b. Did the screen display a warning or ask any questions?

Answers to Odd-Numbered Questions

Key Term Matching Questions

1. k		11. a
3. i		13. t
5. r		15. j
7. h		17. g
9. o		19. s

Multiple-Choice Questions

1. d

3. c

5. e

True/False Questions

1. T

3. T

5. F

Data Files to Active Learning

Exercise	Beginning Name	Ending Name
Directed Exercise		
1	N/A	N/A
2	UNDEL1.TXT UNDEL2.TXT UNDEL3.TXT	UNDEL1.TXT UNDEL2.TXT UNDEL3.TXT
3	UNDEL1.TXT	UNDEL1.TXT

Working with System Information

Chapter Summary

Chapter 12 is the first of three chapters covering the DOS commands and concepts that enable you to change how DOS does its work. This chapter specifically covers the commands that set and retrieve system information, including items such as the date and time maintained by your system, the appearance of your screen, and the commands that enable you to invoke secondary copies of DOS. The following key points are covered in this chapter:

- The DATE and TIME commands alter the date and time used by DOS when you save files to disk.

- The VER command displays the current booted version of DOS.

- The MEM command provides extensive information about the memory, programs, and devices currently running.

- The COMMAND command enables you to execute DOS commands in a different environment or temporarily suspend programs while you use DOS.

- The EXIT command returns you to your program or to the first copy of the command processor.

Chapter Outline

I. Changing the Date and Time

    A. Issuing the DATE Command

    B. Issuing the TIME Command

II. Displaying the Version with VER

III. Setting the Version with SETVER

IV. Displaying the Amount of Free and Used Memory

    A. Issuing the MEM Command

    B. Understanding the Operation of MEM

V. Loading a Secondary Command Processor

    A. Issuing the COMMAND Command

    B. Understanding the Operation of COMMAND

VI. Using EXIT to Leave the Current Copy of the Command Processor

VII. Uses for a Secondary Command Processor

Active Learning

Key Term Matching

Match the following key terms with the definitions listed after them.

____ 1. SETVER		____ 9. VER	
____ 2. TIME		____ 10. MEM /C	
____ 3. EMS		____ 11. UMB	
____ 4. MEM		____ 12. EXIT	
____ 5. SETVER /Q		____ 13. MEM /F	
____ 6. XMS		____ 14. COUNTRY	
____ 7. SETVER /D		____ 15. COMMAND	
____ 8. MEM /P		____ 16. DATE	

12

Definitions

a. Refers to extended memory above 1MB of RAM.

b. This command displays the DOS version currently in use.

c. This command gives a memory report listing the free areas of conventional and upper memory.

d. This DOS internal command can be used to display or change the current date.

e. This command operates as both a device driver and an executable command.

f. Refers to the 384K of memory between 640K and 1M that is usually reserved for use by certain system devices, such as your monitor.

g. This external DOS command enables you to determine how memory is being used on your system.

h. This parameter can be added to the CONFIG.SYS file to change the format used for entering a date or time.

i. This command prevents a warning message from appearing when changing the version table.

j. This internal DOS command can be used to display or change the current time.

k. This command lists programs loaded into conventional memory as well as in upper memory.

l. This command enables you to load a second copy of the system's command processor.

m. This term refers to memory that conforms to the LIM specifications.

n. This command leaves the current copy of the command processor and returns to the previously loaded copy.

o. This command causes your memory report to pause at the end of each screen it displays.

p. This command can be used to delete a program from the DOS 6.2 version list.

Multiple-Choice Questions

____ 1. Using the COMMAND /P command has the effect of

    a. stepping through a specified batch file.
    b. causing DOS to pause at the end of each screenful of display.
    c. making the second copy of the command processor permanent.
    d. causing DOS to permanently load messages into memory instead of reading them from disk every time they are needed.
    e. There is no such option with the COMMAND command.

____ 2. Which of the following is a DOS external command?

    a. VER
    b. MEM
    c. DATE
    d. TIME
    e. These are all internal commands.

____ 3. The command used to add the name of a program to DOS 6.2's version table is:

    a. MEM
    b. VER
    c. COMMAND
    d. SETVER
    e. EXIT

____ 4. The 384K area of memory between 640K and 1MB is called

    a. conventional memory.
    b. EMS.
    c. XMS.
    d. upper memory.
    e. reserved memory.

____ 5. The exact format you should use for entering a date depends on the ____ code set in your CONFIG.SYS file.

    a. country
    b. date
    c. time
    d. device
    e. config

True/False Questions

___ 1. The VER command is an external command that can be used to display the version of DOS currently being used.

___ 2. The switches that might be used with the MEM command are independent and cannot be used together with any other switch except the /P option.

___ 3. The SETVER command operates as both a device driver and an executable command.

___ 4. The EXIT command enables you to temporarily suspend programs while you use DOS.

___ 5. The COMMAND command returns you to the first copy of the command processor.

12

► Directed Exercises

Exercise 1: Practicing Date and Time

In this exercise, you practice using the DATE and TIME commands, entering both correct and incorrect date and time information to compare the results. Follow these steps:

1. At the DOS prompt, type **date** and press **Enter**.

   a. Does the system reflect the correct date?

   b. Press **Enter** to return to the DOS prompt.

2. When you return to the DOS prompt, type **time** and press **Enter**.

   a. Does the system reflect the correct time?

   b. Enter a new valid time by typing **2:00 a** and pressing **Enter**.

   c. What happened? Did the system accept the entry or give you a message?

3. Practice entering a date by again typing **date** and pressing **Enter**. Next, enter an incorrect date by typing **13/32/97** and pressing **Enter**.

   a. What is wrong with this date?

   b. What is the screen's response to your incorrect entry?

4. You should receive the message *Invalid date* and another request to enter a new date. Enter another invalid date by typing **July 4, 1995**.

   a. What is wrong with this new date?

   b. What is the screen's response to your incorrect entry?

5. Enter today's date and press **Enter** to return to the DOS prompt.

6. Enter another valid date using the shortcut method of typing **date 1/1/91**.

7. Practice using the shortcut method to enter several more dates as suggested below or make up your own dates, making a note of which are valid and which are invalid.

   a. 2/30/95

   b. 12-25-94

   c. 11/11/64

   d. 031995

   e. 1/1/80

   f. 5/8/2047

8. Practice using the shortcut method of entering a new time by typing **time 1:30p** and pressing **Enter**. Did the system accept the time entry?

9. Practice using the shortcut method to enter several more times as suggested below or make up your own dates, making a note of which are valid and which are invalid.

   a. 1:04:32.51

   b. 14:30

   c. 2:32:32.32 pm

   d. 12/31:04

   e. 25:25:25.25

   f. 1:1:1:1

Exercise 2: Using VER and SETVER

In this exercise, you practice using the VER and SETVER commands.
Follow these steps:

1. You need to check your CONFIG.SYS file to see if SETVER.EXE is
    currently in it. First make sure that you are in the root directory
    of Drive C: by typing **c:** and pressing **Enter**, and then typing
    cd** and pressing **Enter again.

2. Use the TYPE command to view the contents of the
    CONFIG.SYS file by entering **type config.sys** at the DOS prompt,
    and looking for the line **DEVICE=C:\DOS\SETVER.EXE**. If this
    line is not present in your CONFIG.SYS file, ask your instructor
    for assistance with putting it into the CONFIG.SYS file and then
    reboot your computer.

3. When the computer has been booted with the proper line in the
    CONFIG.SYS file, type **ver** at the DOS prompt and press **Enter** to
    display the version of DOS that is currently in use.

4. Type **setver** at the DOS prompt and press **Enter**.

    a. Was the list of files too long to appear on one screen?

    b. If so, use the command **setver |more** and press **Enter**
        to see each file listed on-screen.

        Note: The | character usually is located above the \ char-
        acter.

    c. Redirect the list to the printer by typing **setver >prn** and
        pressing **Enter**.

        Note: Make sure that your printer is attached and on
        before typing this command.

    d. How many files appear on your list? Do you recognize any
        of them?

    e. Compare your list to the list shown on pages 316 and 317
        of *Using MS-DOS 6.2,* Special Edition.

Exercise 3: Using the MEM Command

In this exercise, you will determine how memory is being used on
your system by practicing several variations on the MEM command.

12

Follow these steps:

1. At the DOS prompt, type **mem** and press **Enter**.

   a. Examine the "short" version of the memory report and compare it to the sample shown on page 320 of *Using MS-DOS 6.2,* Special Edition.

   b. If a printer is available, redirect the report to the printer by typing **mem >prn** and pressing **Enter** to receive a hard copy of your memory information.

2. To get a longer, more technical report on your memory usage, type **mem /c/p** and press **Enter**.

   a. How does the information in this report compare to the short version you received in step 1?

   b. How many "pages" long is this report?

   c. Compare your report to the one shown on pages 323 and 324 of *Using MS-DOS 6.2,* Special Edition.

   d. If a printer is available, redirect output to the printer by typing **mem /c >prn** and pressing **Enter** to receive a hard copy of your longer memory information report.

3. To obtain another highly technical report, type **mem /d/p** and press **Enter.**

   a. How does the information in this report compare to the short version you received in step 1 and the longer version you received in step 2?

   b. How many "pages" long is this report? Is it longer or shorter than the report in step 2?

   c. Does anything in the report make sense to you?

   d. Compare your report to the one shown on pages 321-323 of *Using MS-DOS 6.2,* Special Edition.

   e. If a printer is available, redirect output to the printer by typing **mem /d >prn** and pressing **Enter** to receive a hard copy of your more technical memory information report.

4. To obtain a listing of free memory space without searching through one of the longer reports, type **mem /f** and press **Enter**.

   a. How does the information in this report compare to the short version you received in step 1 and the longer versions you received in steps 2 and 3?

   b. How many "pages" long is this report? Is it longer or shorter than the other reports?

   c. See if you can find the information displayed in this report in one or both of the longer reports obtained in steps 2 and 3.

   d. Compare your report to the one shown on page 325 of *Using MS-DOS 6.2,* Special Edition.

   e. If a printer is available, redirect output to the printer by typing **mem /f >prn** and pressing **Enter** to receive a hard copy of your more technical memory information report.

12

Continuing Problems

Refer to the complete description of the case studies in Chapter 3.

Case Study 1: Burke's Musical Instruments

Shinichi Murakami has been puzzled by a MEMORY FULL message he has received on occasion when using the spreadsheet program. He can't figure out why he would get this message when he has 8MB of memory in the computer. What can he do to analyze the memory usage and possibly solve his problem?

Case Study 2: Medical Offices Of Colby, Odenthal, Bravo & Kim

Rose Smith, a temporary employee working for Dr. Su-Jin Kim, worked on eleven different files yesterday. When Dr. Kim looked at the directory listing of those files, however, the DIR command indicated all the files had been saved with the date of 01-01-80. What might have happened and how can Dr. Kim ensure that the correct date is put on the new files Rose is working on today?

Case Study 3: The DOS Reference Card

In this case study, you continue creating the DOS reference card you began in Chapter 3. Several terms and DOS commands are introduced in this chapter and should be added to the reference card.

Fill in the command, term, or key sequence that matches each description.

Description	Command/Term/Sequence	Type
Enables you to load a second copy of COMMAND.COM.	_____	Command
Changes or displays the correct time.	_____	Command
Returns you to the first copy of the command processor.	_____	Command
Changes or displays the correct date.	_____	Command
Memory between 0K and 640K.	_____	Term
Provides extensive information about memory, programs, and devices currently running.	_____	Command
Displays the current booted version of DOS.	_____	Command

Answers to Odd-Numbered Questions

Key Term Matching Questions

1. e		9. b	
3. m		11. f	
5. i		13. c	
7. p		15. l	

Multiple-Choice Questions

1. c
3. d
5. a

True/False Questions

1. F
3. T
5. F

12

Controlling Your Environment

Chapter Summary

Chapter 13 discusses how you can set system variables and change the DOS prompt. DOS is a full-featured environment that can be used on a variety of computers to run a variety of software programs. Although many people never need to alter the default environment provided by DOS, the commands presented in this chapter can be used to fine-tune DOS to your needs. Chapter 13 explains how to use the MODE command to change how DOS displays information on-screen, as well as how to use DOS to change disk drive configuration.

Chapter 13 covers the following important concepts:

- The SET command enables you to change individual environment variables. These variables include PROMPT, PATH, and COMSPEC.

- The PROMPT command changes the appearance of the command prompt. On systems that use hierarchical directories, changing the prompt setting to PROMPT PG is advisable because it results in the current path always being displayed.

- The MODE command can alter the appearance of the screen. You can alter the number of lines, the number of columns, and the current display.

- The ASSIGN, JOIN, and SUBST commands can redefine how DOS treats your disk drives and subdirectories.

Chapter Outline

I. Changing DOS Variables

    A. Issuing the SET Command
    B. Changing Environment Variables with SET
    C. Defining Your Own Environment Variables with SET

II. Changing the User Interface

    A. Changing the Command Prompt with PROMPT
    B. Altering the Look of the Screen with MODE

III. Changing Disk Drives

    A. The ASSIGN Command
    B. The JOIN Command
    C. The SUBST Command

Active Learning

Key Term Matching

Match the following key terms with the definitions listed after them.

_____ 1. ANSI.SYS	_____ 11. JOIN
_____ 2. $V	_____ 12. VGA
_____ 3. EGA	_____ 13. COMSPEC
_____ 4. $P	_____ 14. User interface
_____ 5. MODE MONO	_____ 15. PROMPT
_____ 6. $B	_____ 16. MODE 80
_____ 7. SET	_____ 17. $G
_____ 8. $D	_____ 18. ASSIGN
_____ 9. Null value	_____ 19. MODE 40
_____ 10. SUBST	_____ 20. $T

Definitions

a. When used with the PROMPT command, displays the vertical bar character (|).

b. Sets the video display to 40 characters per line.

c. This term describes how you (the user) interact with the computer.

d. Replaces a path name for a subdirectory with a drive letter.

e. When used with the PROMPT command, displays the greater-than character (>).

f. This device driver must be installed before MODE can adjust your screen.

g. Enables you to adjust the DOS environment by changing the variables that are available to programs running under DOS.

h. When used with the PROMPT command, displays the time.

i. A type of monitor that uses a Video Graphics Array.

j. When used with the PROMPT command, displays the current path.

k. Assumed when you do not enter a value; in other words, it stands for *nothing*.

l. Sets the video display to 80 characters per line.

m. When used with the PROMPT command, displays the DOS version.

n. This external DOS command can be used to redirect all DOS read-and-write (input-and-output) requests from one drive to another.

o. A reserved system variable name that defines your command processor's location.

p. Sets the video display to monochrome display.

q. Enables you to change what the DOS command prompt looks like.

r. When used with the PROMPT command, displays the system date.

13

s. A type of monitor that uses an Enhanced Graphics Adapter.

t. This command can be used to add a disk drive to the directory structure of another disk.

Multiple-Choice Questions

____ 1. The ____ command is typically used as part of a batch file to establish variables to be used within your system.

   a. ASSIGN
   b. SET
   c. JOIN
   d. MODE
   e. SUBST

____ 2. Which of the following is not a valid PROMPT entry?

   a. PROMPT PG
   b. PROMPT VL
   c. PROMPT Time: THHHHHH_PG
   d. PROMPT DTBM
   e. PROMPT PB$_$G

____ 3. Which of the following commands would set the color display to 40 characters per line?

   a. MODE BW40
   b. MODE 80
   c. MODE CO
   d. MODE MO40
   e. MODE CO40

____ 4. The ____ command allows you to use a floppy disk in such a way that it appears to DOS to be part of a hard disk.

   a. JOIN
   b. ASSIGN /S
   c. SUBST
   d. PROMPT
   e. SET

_____ 5. If you want to run a program that does not support path names, you can use the _____ command to assign a drive letter to a directory.

    a. JOIN
    b. ASSIGN
    c. SUBST
    d. PROMPT
    e. SET

True/False Questions

_____ 1. After you type the command JOIN A: C:\SSDATA, when you access C:\SSDATA you are actually accessing Drive A:.

_____ 2. You should not use the DISKCOPY command with drives that you create with the SUBST command.

_____ 3. If you enter the SET command at the command prompt without any variables, it lists all the current settings for environment variables.

_____ 4. The SUBST command can be used to extend the drive designations set by the LASTDRIVE= parameter in CONFIG.SYS.

_____ 5. The ASSIGN command can be used to redirect all input and output requests from one drive to another as long as each drive is a DOS device.

▶ Directed Exercises

Exercise 1: Set Commands

This exercise is intended to give you practice using variations of the SET command to view and adjust your DOS environment. It assumes that you are starting in the root directory of Drive C: and that you have some SET commands in your AUTOEXEC.BAT file. Follow these steps:

13

1. Examine your AUTOEXEC.BAT file for any SET commands that might exist by entering **type autoexec.bat** at the DOS prompt.

    a. How many SET commands were included in this file?

    b. If a printer is connected to your computer, make sure that the printer's power is on, and then redirect the output to the printer by typing **print autoexec.bat** and pressing **Enter** to obtain a hard copy of the commands included in the AUTOEXEC.BAT file.

2. Now examine the current settings for environment variables directly from the DOS prompt by typing **set** and pressing **Enter**.

    a. How many environment variables were displayed by this command?

    b. Did the output from this command match what you discovered in step 1?

    c. If a printer is connected to your computer and its power is on, redirect the output to the printer by typing **set >prn** and pressing **Enter** to obtain a hard copy of the environment variables displayed by the SET command.

3. Make a particular note of the setting for PROMPT=xxxx by copying it from the screen or marking it on the hard copy of environment settings. Also make a particular note of how the DOS prompt appears on-screen.

4. Use the SET command to change the appearance of the system prompt by typing **set prompt=dt$b** and then press **Enter**. Does the system prompt now appear different than it appeared during step 3?

5. Type **set** one more time and press **Enter**. Compare the current setting for PROMPT=xxxx to what you received in step 3.

6. Use the SET command to return the PROMPT to its original setting.

Exercise 2: Changing the System Prompt's Appearance

In this exercise, you practice modifying the DOS system prompt portion of the user interface. You learn various ways to personalize your system prompt, making it more useful and/or entertaining. This exercise assumes that you are starting at the root directory of Drive C:.

1. Copy what the current DOS prompt looks like on a piece of paper and label the drawing with the numeral 1 to match this step.

2. Change the prompt to the "plain-vanilla" version by typing **prompt** at the DOS command prompt and pressing **Enter**.

    a. Does this appear the same as the prompt in step 1?

    b. Copy the way the DOS prompt looks now onto the same piece of paper and label it *2*.

3. Change your DOS prompt to display today's date with a description of what you are displaying by typing **prompt Today's Date is $d - pg**. Press **Enter**.

    a. How does the prompt compare to the previous two prompts?

    b. Again copy the DOS prompt onto your paper and label it *3*.

4. Try each of the following commands and copy the results onto the piece of paper, labeling them *4a*, *4b*, and so on.

    a. PROMPT DB$_$P$G

    b. PROMPT Buenas Dias!

    c. PROMPT Date: $d Time: t_pg

    d. PROMPT Time: thhhhhhb$g

    e. PROMPT Hello Student!$_What Can I Do For You Today?$_$G

5. Return your system prompt to its original state.

6. What was the difference between changing the prompt in the first exercise and changing it in this exercise?

Exercise 3: Using the Assign Command

In this exercise, you practice using the ASSIGN command. The exercise assumes that you are using a computer with a hard disk designated as Drive C:, that a \DOS subdirectory is on Drive C:, and that you also have a floppy disk drive designated as Drive A:.

13

1. To display a listing of current drive assignments, type **assign /status** and press **Enter**.

    a. Were there any assignments?

    b. If so, copy down what they are.

2. Verify the contents of Drive A: and obtain a hard copy by making sure that the printer is on, and then typing **dir a: >prn** and pressing **Enter**.

3. Verify the contents of Drive C:, and obtain a hard copy by typing **dir c: >prn** and pressing **Enter**.

4. Use the ASSIGN command to redirect all read-and-write requests from your Drive A: floppy disk to the hard disk by typing **assign c:=a:** and then pressing **Enter**.

5. Type **dir a: >prn** and press **Enter**, and then type **dir c: >prn** and press **Enter**.

6. Display a second listing of current drive assignments, type **assign /status** and press **Enter**.

7. Compare the results of steps 5 and 6 to the results obtained in steps 1, 2, and 3.

    a. Were they the same or different?

    b. Make sure that you understand why the results appeared as they did before you continue on.

8. Return all the drive assignments to their original state.

Exercise 4: Customizing the DOS Prompt

The DOS prompt can help you by displaying the full path to your current working directory. In this exercise, change the DOS prompt to display the following variety of prompts. You may want to use the Help command for additional guidance. Print the prompts by using the Print Screen key.

1. [*system date*] [*drive:path*][=]

2. Yes, Master[>]

3. [*system date*], [*system time*][*linefeed*][*drive:path*][>]

4. [*path*] - [*drive:*][$][>]

5. [*drive:path*][>]

Continuing Problems

Refer to the complete description of the case studies in Chapter 3.

Case Study 1: Burke's Musical Instruments

Because it is the time of year many parents buy or rent musical instruments for their school-aged children, Debbie Burke is so busy that she has had to bring in temporary employees to help out. The problem is that many of these temporary employees are not DOS experts and keep getting confused because the accounting program they are using must look for data in the C:\SSDATA directory even though the data is actually stored on a floppy disk that is usually placed in Drive B:. How can Debbie set up her system so that she doesn't have to spend so much time trying to help the temporary employees?

Case Study 2: Medical Offices of Colby, Odenthal, Bravo & Kim

The medical offices are also very busy this time of year, and they have a similar problem. Dr. Odenthal hired extra help to do data entry so that they can get caught up. These temporary employees often need to enter the current date and time into the medical files, but the clock in their office is broken and many employees do not have a watch. Dr. Odenthal heard there is a way to set up the computer system to display the exact time and date but can't remember what to do. What would you recommend if you were asked to help?

Case Study 3: The DOS Reference Card

In this case study, you continue creating the DOS reference card you began in Chapter 3. Several terms and DOS commands are introduced in this chapter and should be added to the reference card. Fill in the command, term, or key sequence that matches each description.

13

Description	Command/Term/Sequence	Type
Replaces a path name for a subdirectory with a drive letter.	_____	Command
Establishes the appearance of the command line prompt.	_____	Command
Modifies the variables used by many DOS commands and other programs running under DOS.	_____	Command
Can customize the number of characters per line and number of lines displayed on-screen.	_____	Command
Redirects all input and output requests from one drive to another.	_____	Command

 # Challenge Problems

1. Leslie Thorson needs to run a program that does not support path names and she needs to assign a drive letter to a specific directory. What command might help her out?

2. What is the difference between the JOIN command and the SUBST command?

Answers to Odd-Numbered Questions

Key Term Matching Questions

1. f	11. t
3. s	13. o
5. p	15. q
7. g	17. e
9. k	19. b

Multiple-Choice Questions

1. b
3. e
5. c

True/False Questions

1. T
3. T
5. T

13

Controlling Devices

Chapter Summary

Chapter 14 explains the DOS commands that control the behavior of logical DOS devices; these commands range from basic commands that clear a screen to advanced filtering and redirection commands. By using these commands, you can control the way DOS sees your system's drives and directories. The chapter also outlines how to use the printer while doing other computer work and how to effectively use the DOS pipes and filters. Chapter 14 covers the following important points:

- Use the CLS command to clear the active display.

- Use the GRAPHICS command to print graphics screens on supported printers.

- The PRINT command is a background printing program.

- Use the CTTY command to change standard input and output devices.

- Use the options available with the MODE command to adjust settings for serial and parallel ports.

- You can use MODE with DOS 4.0, 5.0, and 6.x to alter the keyboard typematic rate.

- You use the MORE, FIND, and SORT filters with text files. The filters are frequently used with redirection and piping.

Chapter Outline

I. The CLS Command

II. The GRAPHICS Command

    A. Issuing the GRAPHICS Command
    B. Using GRAPHICS to Print a Screen Image

III. The PRINT Command

    A. Issuing the PRINT Command
    B. Using PRINT to Print Several Files
    C. General Rules for Using PRINT

IV. The CTTY Command

V. The MODE Command

    A. Using MODE to Change Parallel Port Settings
    B. Using MODE to Change Serial Port Settings
    C. Using MODE to Redirect a Parallel Port to a Serial Port
    D. Issuing the MODE Command to Redirect Ports
    E. Using MODE to Redirect Ports
    F. Using MODE to Change the Typematic Rate

VI. The Redirection Commands

    A. Issuing the Redirection Operators
    B. General Rules for Using Redirection

VII. The MORE Filter

    A. Issuing the MORE Filter
    B. Using MORE to Pause the Screen
    C. General Rules for Using MORE

VIII. The FIND Filter

    A. Issuing the FIND Filter
    B. Using FIND to Find Files on Disk
    C. General Rules for Using FIND

IX. The SORT Filter

    A. Issuing the SORT Filter
    B. Using SORT to Sort Subdirectory Listings
    C. General Rules for Using SORT

Active Learning

Key Term Matching

Match the following key terms with the definitions listed after them.

____ 1. Queue   ____ 11. >>

____ 2. LPT1   ____ 12. CLS

____ 3. Console   ____ 13. GRAPHICS.PRO

____ 4. Input device   ____ 14. MORE

____ 5. FIND   ____ 15. Output device

____ 6. <   ____ 16. |

____ 7. COM1   ____ 17. MODE

____ 8. PRINT   ____ 18. PRN

____ 9. GRAPHICS   ____ 19. >

____ 10. COPY   ____ 20. SORT

Definitions

a. Redirects a command's input.

b. Prints text files in background mode.

c. Any device that you can use to give information to DOS.

d. Passes the output from one command to another as input.

e. Sorts information.

f. A DOS device name indicating the first serial printer.

g. Clears the screen.

h. A DOS device name indicating the first parallel printer.

i. Controls the display of text, showing one screenful at a time.

j. A DOS device name indicating the first printer, which is often a parallel printer.

k. This external DOS command allows you to use the Print Screen key to print graphics screens.

14

l. The place where files wait for a printer when you send multiple files to it.

m. Redirects a command's output.

n. Controls device operations, redirects a parallel port to a serial port, or changes the typematic rate.

o. Finds strings of text.

p. Any device to which DOS can send information.

q. This command is used to select a different console or make the serial port the console.

r. Made up of the combination of your keyboard and screen.

s. Redirects a command's output and appends the output to the target, if one exists.

t. A profile file supplied with DOS.

Multiple-Choice Questions

____ 1. If you use the _____ operator with a DOS command such as DIR, it redirects the command's output and appends the output to the target.

      a. <
      b. >
      c. <<
      d. >>
      e. |

____ 2. The internal DOS command used to remove all visible text from the screen is:

      a. CLS
      b. OFF
      c. MODE
      d. CTTY
      e. MODE CLS

_____ 3. The DOS command that would enable the Print Screen key to output a graphics screen to a printer with a ribbon which prints red, green, blue, and black is:

    a. GRAPHICS
    b. GRAPHICS /4
    c. GRAPHICS COLOR1
    d. GRAPHICS COLOR
    e. GRAPHICS COLOR4

_____ 4. The command and switch used with a monochrome system when you want to print a screen image with the background as black and the text as white is:

    a. GRAPHICS COLOR8 /B
    b. GRAPHICS /R
    c. GRAPHICS COLOR4 /R
    d. GRAPHICS /PRINTBOX:STD
    e. GRAPHICS /B

_____ 5. The command to print the file LETTER.TXT in background mode to the first serial printer is:

    a. COPY LETTER.TXT /D:PRN
    b. COPY LETTER.TXT COM1
    c. PRINT LETTER.TXT COM1
    d. PRINT LETTER.TXT /D:COM1
    e. PRINT LETTER.TXT /D:LPT1

_____ 6. The minimum print buffer size is 512 bytes and the maximum is:

    a. 16K.
    b. 8K.
    c. 1K.
    d. 1M.
    e. 4K.

14

_____ 7. The default queue size is _____ files.

    a. 4
    b. 32
    c. 16
    d. 10
    e. 8

____ 8. The switch used with the PRINT command to stop all printing and remove all files from the queue is:

    a. /P
    b. /Q
    c. /T
    d. /S
    e. /C

____ 9. Which of the following is not an acceptable serial port?

    a. COM1
    b. COM3
    c. COM4
    d. COM2
    e. COM

____ 10. The proper syntax to read the contents of a README.DOC file one page at a time is

    a. TYPE README.DOC | MORE
    b. COPY README.DOC > MORE
    c. TYPE README.DOC > MORE
    d. COPY README.DOC | MORE
    e. MORE >README.DOC

True/False Questions

____ 1. If you use the > operator to redirect output to an existing file, DOS displays a warning message on-screen.

____ 2. Unless you use the /I switch, the FIND command is sensitive to case and discriminates between uppercase and lower-case letters.

____ 3. The CLS command is an internal DOS command that has no switches.

____ 4. The GRAPHICS command allows you to print up to 19 colors on a color printer and up to eight shades of gray on a black-and-white printer.

____ 5. Using the command COPY LETTER.TXT PRN is the same as using the command PRINT LETTER.TXT.

____ 6. The MORE command cannot be used alone because it requires input to redirect or pipe.

_____ 7. You cannot use the /C and /V switches together when using the FIND filter.

_____ 8. You can display all files in the print queue by typing **PRINT** with no switches.

_____ 9. The difference between *baud rate* and *bps* is that *baud rate* specifies the amount of data transferred in a second, and *bps* indicates the signaling rate.

_____10. The command MORE <README.DOC contains proper DOS syntax.

▶ Directed Exercises

Exercise 1: Using Redirection Symbols

This exercise is designed to give you practice using the redirection symbols to change a command's input or output, including appending to an existing file. This exercise requires the data disk and assumes that it is inserted in Drive A:. Make the CH14 subdirectory on Drive A: the default by typing **cd \ch14** and pressing **Enter** before beginning. Follow these steps:

1. Redirect a copy of the directory structure of Drive C: to a file named TEST1 by typing **tree c:\ >test1** and pressing **Enter**.

2. Use the TYPE command to view the contents of the TEST1 file by entering **type test1** and pressing **Enter**.

   a. Did all of the output fit onto one screen?

   b. If not, try the command again by entering **type test1 | more** and pressing **Enter**. How many pages (screens) did it take to display the entire file?

   c. Make a note of the last line displayed from the TEST1 file.

3. Enter the DIR command to see the size of the TEST1 file and write it down.

4. Use the redirection command to append a copy of the directory structure of Drive A: to the end of the file TEST1 by typing **tree a:\ >>test1** and pressing **Enter**.

14

5. Use the TYPE command to view the contents of the TEST1 file a second time by entering **type test1** and pressing **Enter**.

   a. Did all of the output fit onto one screen?

   b. If not, try the command again by entering **type test1 | more** and pressing **Enter**. How many pages (screens) did it take to display the entire file?

   c. Could you see where the first directory structure captured from step 1 ended and where the second directory structure captured in step 4 began?

   d. What is the last line displayed from the TEST1 file? Is it the same as the one you saw in step 2?

6. Use the DIR command again and compare the size of the TEST1 file to the size determined in step 3.

   a. Are they the same? Why or why not?

   b. If one is larger, which one is it?

7. Redirect a copy of the directory listing for the default directory to the file named TEST1 by typing **dir >test1** and pressing **Enter**.

   a. Did you receive a message on-screen warning you that you were about to replace an existing file?

   b. Why or why not?

8. Use the TYPE command to view the contents of the TEST1 file a third time by entering **type test1** and pressing **Enter**.

   a. Did all of the output fit onto one screen?

   b. If not, try the command one more time by entering **type test1 | more** and press **Enter**. How many pages (screens) did it take to display the entire file?

   c. Compare the results of this command to the previous times you looked at the contents of this file. Are they the same?

   d. What is the last line displayed from the TEST1 file? Is it the same as the one you saw in step 2 or step 5?

9. Use the DIR command again and compare the size of the TEST1 file to the size determined in step 3.

   a. Are they the same? Why or why not?

   b. If one is larger, which one is it?

   c. Make sure that you understand what happened to your TEST1 file before continuing.

Exercise 2: Practice Printing

In this exercise, you practice using the various methods DOS provides for printing. To successfully complete this exercise, you need a printer turned on and connected to your computer. The exercise assumes that the printer used is connected to the first parallel port (LPT1). This exercise also requires the data disk and assumes that it is inserted in Drive A:. Make the Ch14 subdirectory on Drive A: the default by typing **cd \ch14** and pressing **Enter** before beginning.

1. From the DOS prompt, print a single file in foreground mode by typing **copy one.txt prn** and pressing **Enter**.

   a. Do you immediately return to the DOS prompt to do other work or do you have to wait until the printing is completed before the DOS prompt appears again?

   b. What message is displayed on-screen, if any?

2. Print the same file in background mode by typing **print one.txt /b:lpt1** and pressing **Enter**.

   a. Do you immediately return to the DOS prompt to do other work or do you have to wait until the printing is completed before the DOS prompt appears again?

   b. What message is displayed on-screen, if any?

   c. Compare this method of printing to that used in step 1. Which method seems faster?

   d. Which method do you prefer?

14

3. Send multiple files to the printer by typing **print *.txt** and pressing **Enter**.

   a. Do you return to the DOS prompt to do other work while the files are printing or do you have to wait until the printing is completed before the DOS prompt appears again?

   b. What message is displayed on-screen, if any?

4. Repeat the above command by pressing the **F3** key, and then pressing **Enter**. Immediately take the printer off-line by pressing the button marked ON-LINE on the printer.

5. Next type the word **print** and press **Enter** again.

   a. Did you get a report of which files were in the print queue and which were printing?

   b. How many files were in the print queue?

   c. Did you get an error message stating that the printer may be off-line?

6. Press the printer's ON-LINE button again, then immediately type **print /t** and press **Enter**.

   a. What happened?

   b. Did a message appear on the screen?

7. Type **print** and press **Enter** again.

   a. How many files were in the print queue?

   b. Did you receive an error message?

   c. Make sure that you understand this command before continuing.

8. Make a list of all the possible ways to print a text file from the command line.

Exercise 3: Using the More Filter

In this exercise, you practice using the DOS filter MORE to modify information as it passes from files to the screen. This exercise also requires the data disk and assumes that the disk is inserted in Drive A:.

It also assumes that you are using a computer with a hard disk designated as Drive C: and that there is a subdirectory on the hard drive named \DOS. Make Drive C: the default drive. Follow these steps:

1. Make the \DOS subdirectory on Drive C: your default directory by typing **cd \dos** at the c:\> prompt.

2. Display a directory listing on the screen by typing **dir** and pressing **Enter**. Be sure not to use any switches when you enter this command.

   a. Did all the file names appear on one screen?

   b. How many files were listed?

   c. If 24 files can appear on one screen, do the arithmetic to determine how many screens would be needed to display the files one screen at a time. How many screens would be required?

3. Enter the DIR command with the /P switch to see if you correctly determined the screen count.

4. Use the MORE filter to pause the next directory listing by typing **dir | more**.

   a. Were the results the same as the results of step 3?

   b. Did you have exactly the same screen count?

5. Now use the TYPE command to view a file that requires more than one screen to display the entire contents by making the CH14 subdirectory on Drive A: the default, and then enter the command **type readme.doc** and press **Enter**.

   a. Did the entire file appear on one screen?

   b. If not, enter the command with the MORE filter by typing **type readme.doc | more** and pressing **Enter**.

   c. How many screens did it take to see the entire file?

6. Use another variation on the MORE filter to redirect the input of the README.DOC file by typing **more <readme.doc**. Be sure to pay attention to which way the redirection symbol is pointing.

14

a. How did this variation compare to the commands entered in step 5?

b. How many screens did it take to see the entire file?

Exercise 4: Using the Find Filter

In this exercise, you practice using the FIND filter and comparing its various options to determine lines in the README.DOC file containing the ASCII string "PRINT". This exercise also requires the data disk and assumes it is inserted in Drive A:. It also assumes you are using a computer with a hard disk designated as Drive C: and that there is a subdirectory on the hard drive named \DOS.

1. Enter the command **find "print" readme.doc**. Make a note of the results.

2. Enter the command **find /c "print" readme.doc**. How do the results compare to step 1?

3. Enter **find /c/i "print" readme.doc**. Were the results the same as in step 2?

4. Enter another variation of the command by typing the following:

   find /n "print" readme.doc

   How do the results compare to steps 1, 2, and 3?

5. Enter **find /n/i "print" readme.doc** and compare the results to all the previous results. Why do they differ?

6. Use the FIND command in combination with the DIR command to find all files on disk that have certain letters or extensions.

   a. Make the root directory on Drive C: your default directory and drive.

   b. Type the command **dir /s /b | find ".ini"** and press **Enter**.

   c. How many files were found?

Exercise 5: Using the Sort Filter

In this exercise, you practice using the SORT filter with the TREE and DIR commands and comparing it to the various switches offered by the DIR command to give similar effects. This exercise assumes that you are using a computer with a hard disk designated as Drive C: and that there is a subdirectory on the hard drive named \DOS. It also assumes that you have a printer powered on and connected to your computer. Follow these steps:

1. Sort the output from the DIR command by file size with the SORT filter and redirect the output to the printer by entering the following command:

    dir c:\dos | sort /+14 > prn

2. Enter the following command:

    dir c:\dos /os > prn

    How do the results compare to step 1?

3. Sort the output from the DIR command by date with the SORT filter and redirect the output to the printer by entering the following command:

    dir c:\dos | sort /+24 > prn

4. Enter the following command:

    dir c:\dos /od > prn

    How do the results compare to step 3?

5. Create a sorted list of subdirectories in the root directory and redirect it to a file by typing the following:

    tree c:\ /a | sort > temp.lst

6. Use the TYPE command to view the contents of the TEMP.LST file.

    a. Did the complete contents of the TEMP.LST file appear on one screen?

    b. If not, use the MORE filter to display the contents one screen at a time.

14

Continuing Problems

Refer to the complete description of the case studies in Chapter 3.

Case Study 1: Burke's Musical Instruments

Pamela Oropeza can't remember which file name she used when she saved an important file about six months ago, or exactly when it was last saved. She does remember that the file referred to the country "Bolivia" several times and is sure that it would be the only file with that word in the text. What should Pamela type to find the file?

Case Study 2: Medical Offices of Colby, Odenthal, Bravo & Kim

Dr. Patricia Bravo has started using the computer a lot since it was installed. She has personally created about 75 files in 14 directories and would like to print a record of her personal directory structure. She also would like to keep a file on disk that contains a copy of how the directory structure and file names look today so that she can compare it to how it evolves over the next six months. What can Dr. Bravo do to accomplish her goals?

Case Study 3: The DOS Reference Card

In this case study, you continue creating the DOS reference card you began in Chapter 3. Several terms and DOS commands are introduced in this chapter and should be added to the reference card.

Fill in the command, term, or key sequence that matches each description.

Description	Command/Term/Sequence	Type
Any device to which DOS can send information.	_____	Term
Clears the screen.	_____	Command
Selects a different console or makes the serial port the console.	_____	Command
Controls the display of text.	_____	Filter
Redirects a command's output.	_____	Operator
Enables you to use the Print Screen key to print graphics screens to a printer.	_____	Command
Sends jobs to the print queue so they can print in the background.	_____	Command
Controls device operations, redirects a parallel port to a serial port, changes the typematic rate.	_____	Command

Challenge Problems

14

1. Jean Gillis needs to create a single file that shows the entire tree structure on her computer and all file names, first sorted by size and then sorted by date. What commands would she enter to create a file called TREE.TXT and append all of the variations she needs to see?

2. Jean's daughter, Colleen, recently purchased a new serial printer for her mother. Jean now needs to adjust the serial port COM3 to 9600 baud rate, parity off, 8 databits, 1 stopbit, with a continuous retry. What should she type at the command line?

3. Javier Mendoza wants to set his keyboard so that the delay before the key repeats is one-half second with a repeat rate of 30 characters per second. What should he enter to make this change to his system?

Answers to Odd-Numbered Questions

Key Term Matching Questions

1.	l	11.	s
3.	r	13.	t
5.	o	15.	p
7.	q	17.	n
9.	k	19.	m

Multiple-Choice Questions

1.	d	7.	d
3.	e	9.	e
5.	d		

True/False Questions

1.	F	7.	F
3.	T	9.	F
5.	F		

Data Files to Active Learning

Exercise	Beginning Name	Ending Name
Directed Exercise		
1	TEST1	TEST1
2	ONE.TXT TWO.TXT THREE.TXT FOUR.TXT	ONE.TXT TWO.TXT THREE.TXT FOUR.TXT
3	README.DOC	README.DOC
4	README.DOC	README.DOC
5	TEMP.LST	TEMP.LST

14

Using the DOS Editor

Chapter Summary

Chapter 15 is the first of five chapters providing the information needed to tap the expanded power available with DOS. This chapter provides a tutorial approach to the built-in text-file editor that comes with DOS. The examples developed in this chapter demonstrate how to use the DOS Editor as a day-to-day utility.

The DOS Editor is a text processor, a kind of mini word processor. The Editor is the perfect tool for creating short text files, memos, and batch files. The chapter explains how to use the basic features of the DOS Editor, including how to use its menus and shortcut commands and how to create, edit, save, and print text.

The chapter covers the following concepts and skills:

- Navigating the menus and dialog boxes of the DOS Editor
- Basic editing techniques in the Editor
- Editing blocks of text
- Searching for and replacing selected text
- Managing files through the Editor
- Customizing your screen in the Editor

Chapter Outline

I. Understanding the DOS Editor

    A. Uses for the DOS Editor
    B. Files Required to Run the DOS Editor
    C. Starting the DOS Editor
    D. Getting Acquainted with the Initial Editor Screen

II. Navigating the DOS Editor

    A. Understanding the Menu System
    B. Understanding Dialog Boxes
    C. Using Shortcut Keys
    D. Using a Mouse

III. Mastering Fundamental Editing Techniques

    A. Moving the Cursor
    B. Scrolling
    C. Inserting Text into a Line
    D. Deleting Text from a Line
    E. Splitting and Joining Lines
    F. Inserting and Deleting an Entire Line
    G. Overtyping

IV. Learning Special Editing Techniques

    A. Using Automatic Indent
    B. Using Tab
    C. Using Place Markers

V. Block Editing

    A. Selecting Text
    B. Understanding the Clipboard
    C. Working with Text Blocks

VI. Searching and Replacing

    A. Using the Find Command
    B. Using the Change Command

VII. Managing Files

    A. Introducing the File Menu
    B. Saving a File
    C. Using the Save As Command
    D. Using the Open Command to Load a File
    E. Loading a File When You First Start the DOS Editor

Active Learning

Key Term Matching

Match the following key terms with the definitions listed after them.

_____ 1.	Tab	_____11.	Enter
_____ 2.	Text Editor	_____12.	Ctrl-Ins
_____ 3.	README	_____13.	Ctrl-S
_____ 4.	Menu bar	_____14.	Overtype
_____ 5.	F6	_____15.	F3
_____ 6.	EDIT	_____16.	Scroll bar
_____ 7.	Text string	_____17.	Escape
_____ 8.	Ctrl-Y	_____18.	Clipboard
_____ 9.	Dialog box	_____19.	Alt-Plus
_____10.	Shift-Ins	_____20.	Status bar

Definitions

a. The "go ahead" key; press it when you are ready to execute a command.

b. A sequence of one or more consecutive text characters, including letters, digits, punctuation, or special symbols.

15

c. This shortcut key enlarges the active window.

d. A program that works with files that contain pure text.

e. This key can be used to abort a menu option and return you to the Editor.

f. The bar at the top of the Editor screen that lists the available menus such as File, Edit, Search, Options, and Help.

g. This shortcut key pastes text from the Clipboard.

h. This key moves the cursor from one area of the dialog box to the next area.

i. This shortcut key repeats the last find.

j. The bar at the bottom of the screen which describes the current process and shows certain shortcut key options.

k. This key combination deletes an entire line.

l. In this mode, any new character you type replaces the character at the cursor location.

m. A file that explains the contents of other files in the subdirectory or on the disk.

n. A reserved area of memory that stores for later use the most recent text that has been copied or cut.

o. This key combination moves the cursor one character to the left.

p. A vertical strip along the right edge or a horizontal strip at the bottom of the screen; used with a mouse to move through the file.

q. This shortcut key moves between Help and the last active window.

r. This shortcut key will copy selected text.

s. The external DOS command that brings up the text editor program.

t. An on-screen box that asks you to enter further information before carrying out the requested function.

Multiple-Choice Questions

____ 1. Which of the following would not be a typical task for the DOS Editor?

    a. writing programs for programming language environments that don't include a resident editor

    b. creating and editing binary files which contain programming instructions or formatted data

    c. viewing text files whose contents are unknown

    d. creating or modifying various system configuration files

    e. writing and modifying batch files

____ 2. The vertical strip along the right edge of the Editor screen is used to

    a. list the available menus.

    b. display the name of the text file being edited.

    c. move through the file by using a mouse.

    d. describe the current process.

    e. show certain shortcut key options.

____ 3. The key(s) to display the File menu is/are

    a. F.

    b. Ctrl-F.

    c. Shift-F.

    d. Alt-S.

    e. Alt-F.

____ 4. The "oops" key that closes the menu system and returns you to the Editor is

    a. Enter.

    b. Ctrl-Q.

    c. Ctrl-Escape.

    d. Escape.

    e. Ins.

____ 5. The ____ temporarily stores a block of text in a reserved area of memory.

    a. text string

    b. text block

    c. Clipboard

    d. paste zone

    e. copy buffer

15

____ 6. To scroll one window left, use the following key combination:

    a. Ctrl-PgUp
    b. Ctrl-PgDn
    c. Ctrl-up arrow
    d. Ctrl-Z
    e. Ctrl-W

____ 7. To move the cursor to the beginning of text, use the following key combination:

    a. Ctrl-Home
    b. Home-Up arrow
    c. Shift-PgUp
    d. Ctrl-PgUp
    e. Shift-Ctrl-Home

____ 8. Which of the following shortcut keys will not affect the contents of the Clipboard?

    a. Del
    b. Ctrl-Ins
    c. Shift-Ins
    d. Shift-Del
    e. All of these shortcut keys will affect the contents of the Clipboard.

____ 9. Which of the following File menu commands clears the file currently in the DOS Editor, resulting in a clean slate as though you had just initialized the Editor?

    a. Save
    b. Print
    c. Open
    d. New
    e. Exit

____10. When you start the DOS Editor, the _____ special parameter switch displays the maximum number of lines possible with your video hardware.

    a. /C
    b. /N
    c. /H
    d. /G
    e. /B

True/False Questions

_____ 1. After you start the DOS Editor, pressing Escape activates the Survival Guide that provides help for using the DOS Editor.

_____ 2. The DOS Editor menu bar contains the File, Edit, Search, Options, and Help options.

_____ 3. When you press the Del key, the selected text is deleted from the file and placed in the Clipboard.

_____ 4. The Shift-Ins shortcut key copies selected text into the Clipboard.

_____ 5. If you don't specify another extension, the Editor adds the extension TXT to the file name when you save a file.

_____ 6. Pressing the Ins key toggles the user between Overtype mode and Insert mode.

_____ 7. When a DOS Editor dialog box opens, the Tab key moves the cursor from one area of the dialog box to the next area.

_____ 8. The Save As dialog box is used when you first save a file or when you save a file under a new name.

_____ 9. The Clipboard can contain one or more blocks of text, which can be added, subtracted, or moved incrementally.

_____ 10. To move between Help and the desired window, use the F6 shortcut key.

▶ # Directed Exercises

Exercise 1: Getting Acquainted with the DOS Editor Screen

Familiarize yourself with the different areas of the DOS Editor. Locate the following areas and briefly describe each:

1. Horizontal scroll bar

2. Vertical scroll bar

3. Title bar

15

4. Menu bar

5. Status bar

6. Editor window

Exercise 2: Using the DOS Editor File Menu

This exercise gives you practice using the commands listed on the File menu. It assumes that you are starting the DOS Editor from Drive C: and requires you to place the Activities disk in Drive A:. Follow these steps:

1. At the DOS Prompt, type **edit** and press **Enter** to start the DOS Editor.

2. Display the list of menu options by pressing the **Alt** key once. Locate the letters that are a different color from the other characters. Choose **F**ile **O**pen.

3. Press **Alt-D** to change the drive/directory. *Hint:* The cursor will blink under the first directory listed but will not highlight that directory until you use the down-arrow key or press the space bar.

4. Change the drive and/or directory so that you can use the data disk and the current directory is CHAP15.

    a. How many files are listed?

    b. What are the file names?

    c. Print a listing of the file names.

5. Choose the **New** command from the **F**ile menu to create a new file.

    a. What name is displayed in the title bar?

    b. Enter the following six lines of text exactly as shown:

    This line demonstrates the Clear command.

    This line demonstrates the Cut command.

    This line demonstrates the Copy command.

    This line demonstrates the Find command.

    This line demonstrates the Find Again command.

    This line demonstrates the Change command.

6. Save the new text as **PRACTICE.TXT** on Drive A: by choosing File **S**ave and then choosing Drive A:. Finally, type the file name.

7. Print PRACTICE.TXT by choosing **P**rint from the **F**ile menu. Make sure that the printer is on.

8. Choose **N**ew from the **F**ile menu as if you were going to create a new file, and then choose the **O**pen command from the **F**ile menu.

   a. What file is listed?

   b. Explain how you can list other files that do not end with a TXT extension.

9. Choose Cancel to abort opening a file. Explain the difference between the Save command and the Save As command.

Exercise 3: Using the DOS Editor Edit Menu

In this exercise, you practice with the commands listed on the Edit menu. It assumes that you have completed exercise 2. Follow these steps:

1. Using the PRACTICE.TXT file, place the cursor in row 1, column 1 (it should be under the T of the word) and press **Enter** three times. What action was performed?

2. Block the line of text that relates to the Clear command and press **Del**.

   a. Does the Paste command enable you to recover what you deleted?

   b. What should you do to revert back to the way the text was before you pressed the Del key?

3. Select the line of text that relates to the Cut command. Cut and paste this text to the top of the file, which begins at row 1, column 1.

   a. Does the text appear as it was previously?

   b. Explain why this feature would be useful for text files.

15

4. Select the line of text that relates to the Copy command. Copy and paste this text under the preceding line (row 2, column 1).

   a. Explain how this feature would be useful for text files.

   b. Why would you want to duplicate a line or more of text?

   c. Print a hard copy of the screen display.

5. Three blank lines separate the first two lines of text from the remaining text. Use the **Shift** and arrow keys to block these blank lines.

6. Delete these blank lines. You should have a total of six lines of text.

7. Save and print this file.

Exercise 4: Using the DOS Editor Search Menu

In this exercise, you practice using the commands listed on the Search menu. This exercise assumes that you have completed exercises 2 and 3. Follow these steps:

1. Open the PRACTICE.TXT file, if it is not already open.

2. Using the **Find** command, search for the word *FIND*.

   a. What happens when the word is found?

   b. What precautions should you take after a word has been found?

3. Press the **F3** key. What action is performed when using the F3 key?

4. Press **F3** again. What action is performed?

5. Search for the word *FOUND*. What message is displayed?

6. Search for the words *LINE DEMONSTRATES* and change them to *LINE WILL DEMONSTRATE*. This change should affect all occurrences. How can you change every other occurrence?

7. Save and print this file.

Exercise 5: DOS Editor Editing Techniques

In this exercise, you practice using indents and place markers, as well as other editing techniques. This exercise assumes that you have completed the other exercises in this chapter. Follow these steps:

1. Open the file in the CHAP15 directory called SUMMARY.TXT. This file may be somewhat hard to read because the lines of text are longer than the width of the screen.

2. Move the cursor to the right edge of the screen where there is a space between words, and press **Enter** to break this line into two separate lines of text.

3. Break the remaining lines of text using the technique in step 2. When you finish, you should be able to read the text without having to scroll to the right.

4. Find the first occurrence of a colon (:).

   a. Holding down **Ctrl**, press and release the letter **K**, and release **Ctrl**.

   b. Press **1** (the number one key).

   c. What function or procedure did you just perform?

5. Search for the word *TAB*.

   a. Perform the same function as before using **Ctrl-K**, but this time press **2** (the number two key).

   b. If you want to go quickly back to place marker 1, what keystrokes can you use?

6. Four keys points are listed, each indicated by an asterisk. Two additional key points that should be added follow.

   a. Position the cursor at the end of the last key point, and then press **Enter**.

   b. Where is the cursor?

   c. Enter the following two key points:

      Managing files through the DOS Editor.

      Customizing your screen in the Editor.

15

7. The last key point is missing some text.

   a. Insert the word *DOS* before the word *Editor*.

   b. What key should you press to activate Overtype mode?

   c. What key do you press to activate Insert mode?

   d. Save and print this file.

 # Continuing Problems

Refer to the complete description of the case studies in Chapter 3.

Case Study 1: Burke's Musical Instruments

Debbie Burke and her employees often need to write a quick note to their customers. Debbie decided to purchase a word processing program. However, when she saw how expensive they were at the computer store, she decided to investigate other possibilities. What would you suggest for the company? What would be the advantages and disadvantages of using the DOS Editor for this task?

Case Study 2: Medical Offices of Colby, Odenthal, Bravo & Kim

Dr. Bravo was experimenting with the COPY command and accidentally added the contents of another file to the AUTOEXEC.BAT file. When she started her computer system, strange things seemed to happen, and some applications do not seem to be working anymore.

Dr. Bravo's patient, Yvan Rodriguez, who is a computer consultant, happened to be in the office and offered assistance. He used the TYPE command to display the contents of AUTOEXEC.BAT and saw that the contents of a file were added to the AUTOEXEC.BAT file. He knew that this problem is easily fixed and simply required editing the AUTOEXEC.BAT file to remove the unwanted contents.

He typed **edit** to start the DOS Editor, but an error message appeared: `Cannot find file QBASIC.EXE`. The DOS Editor does not seem to be working. Yvan checked the path and directory listing for the

EDIT.EXE file. Everything seems to be in order. What could be causing this problem? DOS 6.2 is the operating system loaded on this computer. How can Yvan fix this problem?

Case Study 3: The DOS Reference Card

In this case study, you continue creating the DOS reference card you began in Chapter 3. Several terms and DOS commands are introduced in this chapter and should be added to the reference card. Fill in the command, term, or key sequence that matches each description.

Description	Command/Term/Sequence	Type
A window that pops open when the DOS Editor needs more information before executing a command.		Term
A line across the top of the screen that lists the available menus.		Term
The large area in which the text of your file appears.		Term
The inverse-video rectangle inside the vertical or horizontal scroll bar.		Term
A sequence of one or more consecutive text characters.		Term
Deletes selected text from the file; the contents of the Clipboard are not affected.		Command
Closes the Editor and returns to where it was started.		Command
Searches for the text specified in the last Find command.		Command
Places in the Clipboard a copy of selected text from a file.		Command

15

(continues)

Description	Command/Term/Sequence	Type
A shortcut key used to activate the Help menu.	_____	Sequence
A shortcut key used to delete selected text from a file; places that text in the Clipboard.	_____	Sequence
Loads a specified file into the Editor for editing.	_____	Command
Searches for specific text and replaces it with specified text.	_____	Command
Used for storing a file for the first time and for saving a second version of a file.	_____	Command
Temporarily stores a block of text in reserved memory.	_____	Term

 # Challenge Problems

1. From within the DOS Editor, you can cut and paste text from and to different locations in the file you are working with. This feature uses the Clipboard to store the text temporarily. Windows programs use a Clipboard for copying and pasting, just like the DOS Editor uses the Clipboard. The problem is that the DOS Editor is not a Windows program. You can copy and paste text from a Windows program to the DOS Editor, however. Explain how you can accomplish this process.

2. Embret Anderson has been using the DOS Shell and has become comfortable using it. When he turns on his computer, he types **dosshell** to start the DOS Shell at the DOS prompt. Embret's cousin Justin has his computer set up to make the DOS Shell come up automatically instead of entering it at the DOS prompt. Explain how Justin can have the DOS Shell come up automatically when he starts his computer, but Embret has to enter it each time.

Answers to Odd-Numbered Questions

Key Term Matching Questions

1.	h	11.	a
3.	m	13.	o
5.	q	15.	i
7.	b	17.	e
9.	t	19.	c

Multiple-Choice Questions

1.	b	7.	a
3.	e	9.	d
5.	c		

True/False Questions

1.	F	7.	T
3.	F	9.	F
5.	F		

Data Files to Active Learning

Exercise	Beginning Name	Ending Name
Directed Exercise		
2	PRACTICE.TXT	PRACTICE.TXT
3	PRACTICE.TXT	PRACTICE.TXT
4	PRACTICE.TXT	PRACTICE.TXT
5	SUMMARY.TXT	SUMMARY.TXT

15

Understanding Batch Files

Chapter Summary

Chapter 16 guides you through the process of creating batch files and keystroke macros. The commands related to batch files are explained in a tutorial style, making it easier to master the basics of batch files. A batch file is a text (ASCII) file containing a series of commands that you want DOS to execute. When you type the batch file name, DOS executes these commands in the order they occur within the batch file. This chapter explains how to create and use DOS batch files.

Batch files and macros can make your computer do the hard work for you, replacing repetitive typing with commands that execute automatically. When you work with batch files and macros, remember the following key points:

- Batch files must have the file extension BAT.

- Batch files are invoked by typing the name of the batch file (without the extension) and pressing Enter. You can specify an optional drive name and path name before the batch file name.

- Any command can be included in a batch file that can be typed at the DOS prompt.

- Each word (or set of characters) in a command separated by a delimiter is a parameter. When you use a batch file, DOS substitutes the appropriate parameters for the variable markers (%0 through %9) in the file.

- The ECHO command can be used to turn on or off the display of DOS commands being executed by the batch file.

- The @ character suppresses the display of a single line from a batch file.

- The PAUSE command causes the batch file to suspend execution and then displays a message on-screen.

- The REM command can be used to leave comments and reminders in a batch file; the comments do not appear on-screen when ECHO is off.

- The GOTO command can be used to change how a batch file executes.

- An IF statement tests for a given condition.

- The CHOICE command enables you to prompt for input and create menus.

- FOR..IN..DO can repeat a batch file command for one or more files or commands.

- SHIFT moves command parameters to the left.

- COMMAND/C and CALL invoke a second batch file and then return control of the computer to the first batch file.

Chapter Outline

I. Introducing Batch Files

II. Understanding the Contents of Batch Files

III. Creating a Simple Batch File

IV. Understanding Replaceable Parameters

V. Using Batch File Commands

VI. Displaying Messages and Inserting Comments

VII. Branching with GOTO

VIII. Using the IF Command

     A. Using IF to Test ERRORLEVEL
     B. Using IF to Compare Strings
     C. Using IF to Look for Files

IX. Pausing for Input in a Batch File

     A. Making a Two-Way Choice
     B. Creating a Simple Menu
     C. Creating a Simple Display Menu

X. Using FOR..IN..DO

     A. Using a FOR..IN..DO Batch File
     B. Using FOR..IN..DO at the DOS Prompt
     C. Using FOR..IN..DO with Other Commands

XI. Moving Parameters with SHIFT

XII. Running Batch Files from Other Batch Files

     A. Shifting Control Permanently to Another Batch File
     B. Calling a Batch File and Returning Using CALL
     C. Using COMMAND.COM to Execute a Batch File

Active Learning

Key Term Matching

Match the following key terms with the definitions listed after them.

____ 1. PAUSE	____11. CHOICE /S
____ 2. ERRORLEVEL	____12. GOTO
____ 3. %1	____13. Ctrl-C
____ 4. Infinite loop	____14. @
____ 5. IF	____15. FOR...IN...DO
____ 6. ECHO OFF	____16. CHOICE /N
____ 7. F6	____17. :END
____ 8. REM	____18. CALL
____ 9. Batch file	____19. SHIFT
____10. ASCII	____20. ECHO

Definitions

a. This batch file command permits conditional execution of a command.

b. A special command included in batch files that runs another batch file and then returns to the original batch file.

c. This key combination stops the execution of a batch file.

d. A batch file command that displays a message and halts processing until a key is pressed.

e. A text file containing a series of commands that you want DOS to execute.

f. Used to display a text message on-screen.

g. This command can be used to decide whether to process certain commands and instructs the command to pay attention to the case of the key pressed.

h. Puts the end-of-file marker on files created with COPY CON.

i. The first replaceable parameter, also called a variable.

j. This batch file command permits the use of the same batch command for several files (the execution *loops*).

k. A batch file command that moves the command-line parameter one parameter to the left.

l. All batch files must be in this format.

m. A program that never stops on its own; it must be manually halted.

n. This command can be used to decide whether to process certain commands and prevents the display of acceptable keys at the end of the prompt.

o. This command enables you to insert comments into a batch file that describe the purpose of an operation.

p. A code left by a program when it finishes executing.

q. Stops the display of the current line.

r. This label is often used to mark the end of a batch file.

s. This command jumps to the line following the specified label in a batch file.

t. Stops the display of all subsequent lines.

Multiple-Choice Questions

____ 1. You can stop a batch file by pressing:

        a. Ctrl-Z

        b. Ctrl-Q

        c. Escape

        d. Ctrl-Escape

        e. Ctrl-C

____ 2. To suppress the display of the current line in a batch file, use the _____ command.

        a. %1

        b. "

        c. :

        d. @

        e. ECHO OFF

____ 3. The _____ command jumps to the line following the specified label in a batch file.

        a. SHIFT

        b. GOTO

        c. REM

        d. PAUSE

        e. CHOICE

____ 4. A replaceable parameter can be put in your batch file by preceding the variable name with the _____ character.

        a. @

        b. #

        c. %

        d. ^

        e. :

____ 5. The _____ command enables you to insert comments into a batch file that describe the purpose of an operation.

        a. CALL

        b. CHOICE

        c. SHIFT

        d. GOTO

        e. REM

____ 6. The ____ command runs another batch file and returns to the original batch file.

    a. CALL
    b. CHOICE
    c. SHIFT
    d. GOTO
    e. REM

____ 7. A batch file label is a separate line that is not a command and consists of a ____ followed by one to eight characters.

    a. %
    b. ^
    c. @
    d. :
    e. !

____ 8. The ERRORLEVEL exit code of ____ usually indicates that the command was successful.

    a. 0
    b. 1
    c. 2
    d. 3
    e. 4

____ 9. The ERRORLEVEL exit code of ____ indicates a "fatal" read/write error occurred and terminated the copy procedure before it was completed.

    a. 0
    b. 1
    c. 2
    d. 3
    e. 4

____ 10. A command that does the same thing as CALL is:

    a. CHOICE
    b. COMMAND /C
    c. SHIFT
    d. GOTO
    e. IF

True/False Questions

_____ 1. If you don't specify which keys should be pressed, CHOICE assumes Y and N.

_____ 2. You can use the ECHO command to turn on or off the display of DOS commands being executed by the batch file.

_____ 3. A batch file can include any program name you usually type at the DOS command line but the file name cannot be the same as a program file name (that is, any file with an EXE or COM extension).

_____ 4. You can use the GOTO command to test for a given condition.

_____ 5. SHIFT moves command parameters to the right.

_____ 6. Batch files can be created with the DOS Editor, Edlin, COPY CON, or any word processor as long as the file is saved in ASCII format.

_____ 7. Use the PAUSE command to leave comments and reminders in your batch file which do not appear on-screen when ECHO is off.

_____ 8. IF...THEN...ELSE can repeat a batch file command for one or more files or commands.

_____ 9. The @ character suppresses the display of all subsequent lines in a batch file.

_____ 10. The CALL command is the same as the CHOICE command.

▶ Directed Exercises

Exercise 1: Displaying Batch File Contents

This exercise is designed to give you practice viewing the contents of batch files. It assumes that you are using a computer with a hard disk designated as Drive C:, and that there is a batch file called AUTOEXEC.BAT in the root directory of Drive C:. Follow these steps:

1. When you boot your computer, go to the root directory of Drive C: by first typing **c:** and pressing **Enter**, and then typing **cd** and pressing **Enter** again.

2. Enter the command **TYPE AUTOEXEC.BAT** and press **Enter.**

   a. Did all of the lines appear on the screen? If not, re-enter the command with the |**MORE** filter.

   b. How many lines are in this file?

   c. Do you recognize any of the commands?

   d. Look up any commands that you do not recognize in the Command Reference section of *Using MS-DOS 6.2,* Special Edition.

3. Use the FIND command to locate any other files with the BAT extension on Drive C: and redirect the output to the printer. *Note:* Make sure that a printer is attached to your computer and turned on before completing this command.

4. Use the TYPE command to view the contents of these files and compare them to the AUTOEXEC.BAT file. Ask the following questions for each batch file:

   a. Did all of the lines appear on-screen? If not, re-enter the command with the |**MORE** filter.

   b. How many lines are in this file?

   c. Do you recognize any of the commands?

   d. Look up any commands that you do not recognize in the Command Reference section of *Using MS-DOS 6.2,* Special Edition.

Exercise 2: Creating and Using Batch Files

In this exercise, you practice creating and using a simple batch file. Batch files are used every day for different purposes. Batch files are used to execute multiple commands from a single command name. Usually, batch files are created for repetitive purposes, such as AUTOEXEC.BAT. Follow these steps:

1. Create a batch file called EASY.BAT by using the DOS Editor or COPY CON. Have the batch file clear the screen and echo *HELLO* to the screen.

2. Execute EASY.BAT and then print its contents.

3. Modify EASY.BAT using the DOS Editor or EDLIN to have it perform a few more commands as follows:

   @ECHO OFF

   CLS

   ECHO HELLO %1

4. Execute EASY.BAT, and type your name as a parameter.

   a. What is the difference between the first time EASY.BAT was executed and now?

   b. Would the results be the same if you did not use the variable %1?

5. Add the following lines to the end of EASY.BAT:

   PAUSE

   IF EXIST \AUTOEXEC.BAT GOTO CLOSE

   ECHO FILE NOT FOUND

   GOTO END

   :CLOSE

   CLS

   ECHO AUTOEXEC.BAT FILE IS IN THE ROOT DIRECTORY

   :END

6. Explain each line of EASY.BAT.

   a. Name the six batch file commands that are used in EASY.BAT.

   b. Print the contents of EASY.BAT.

Exercise 3: Practicing Batch Files with the GOTO Command

In this exercise, you practice using the GOTO command in batch files. You will create a file that contains an infinite loop that must be halted with the Ctrl-C (or Ctrl-Break) command. Follow these steps:

1. Using the DOS Editor, EDLIN, or the COPY CON command, create the following batch file and save it with the name **LOOP.BAT**.

   @ECHO OFF

   :LOOP

       ECHO Hello, %1

       PAUSE

   GOTO LOOP

2. To test the batch file, type the name of the file followed by a space and your name. For example, student Qasim Baqai would type **loop qasim** and press **Enter.**

3. Did the screen greet you and then wait for you to press a key?

4. When you pressed a key, did the same message appear again?

5. Stop the batch file by pressing **Ctrl-C.**

6. Explain how the batch file worked and why the same message kept appearing again.

Exercise 4: Practice with AUTOEXEC.BAT

In this exercise, you practice creating and executing an AUTOEXEC.BAT file. This exercise assumes that you are using a computer with a hard disk designated as Drive C: and that there is an existing AUTOEXEC.BAT file in the root directory of Drive C:. Follow these steps:

1. When you boot your computer, go to the root directory of Drive C: by typing **c:** and pressing **Enter**, then typing **cd** and pressing **Enter** again.

2. Enter the command **ren autoexec.bat autoexec.old** and press **Enter**. *This step is very important; be sure you complete it before continuing.*

3. Enter an AUTOEXEC.BAT batch file that accomplishes the following:

   a. Suppresses the commands from appearing on-screen.

   b. Sets a PATH to the root of Drive C: and to the C:\DOS subdirectory.

   c. Displays the current path in the system prompt.

   d. Sets a temporary directory to C:\DOS.

   e. Sets the DATE and TIME according to two variable inputs entered when you execute the command.

   f. Greets you by name.

   g. Includes a choice of whether to bring up the DOS Shell.

4. Test the file by typing AUTOEXEC at the command line.

   a. Did the file work as expected?

   b. If not, fix any errors that occurred and retest the command.

5. Make sure that the file automatically executes by pressing Ctrl-Alt-Del to warm boot the computer.

6. When you have made sure the file works properly, copy it to your Activities disk.

7. VERY IMPORTANT STEP: Restore the original AUTOEXEC.BAT file by typing **ren autoexec.old autoexec.bat** before continuing.

Exercise 5: Working with More Complex Batch Files

In this exercise, you practice working with a more complex batch file. The purpose of the batch file is to make disk copies in Drive A: by using the DISKCOPY command and the verify option. If the diskcopy procedure terminates before completion, you want the batch file to inform you of the cause. Follow these steps:

1. Create a batch file named DCOPY.BAT that contains the following lines:

```
@ECHO OFF
DISKCOPY A: A: /V
IF ERRORLEVEL 4 GOTO INIT_ERR
IF ERRORLEVEL 3 GOTO FATL_ERR
IF ERRORLEVEL 2 GOTO CTRL-C
IF ERRORLEVEL 1 GOTO NON_FATL
ECHO DISKCOPY successful and verified!
GOTO END
:INIT_ERR
    ECHO Initialization error!
    GOTO END
```

```
        :FATL_ERR
              ECHO Fatal error! DISKCOPY stopped!
              GOTO END
        :CTRL-C
              ECHO Someone pressed Ctrl-C!
              GOTO END
        :NON_FATL
              ECHO A non-fatal error occurred. Check data!
        :END
```

2. Test the batch file by typing **dcopy** at the command line and then press **Enter**.

    a. Did you get prompted to Insert SOURCE diskette in drive A?

    b. Complete the diskcopy procedure and see if it works.

3. Why are the tests listed in descending order?

 # Continuing Problems

Refer to the complete description of the case studies in Chapter 3.

Case Study 1: Burke's Musical Instruments

Pamela Oropeza wants a simple batch file to perform a Copy and Delete function with directories. In other words, she wants to create a new directory, move the contents of another directory to the new directory, delete the contents of the old directory, and, finally, re-move the old directory. Being an experienced DOS user, Pamela knows that only the COPY, DEL, MD, and RD commands are needed. Write a simple batch file that uses replaceable parameters to copy a source to a destination and then deletes the source. This file should be called MOVEDIR.BAT. Print the contents of MOVEDIR.BAT.

Case Study 2: Medical Offices of Colby, Odenthal, Bravo & Kim

Dr. Colby's daughter takes music lessons at Burke's Musical Instruments, and she saw their MOVEDIR.BAT file. She wants a similar file but with enhancements to check for the source file by using the IF command to see whether the file exists. She also wants to perform error-level checks. In order to check error-level codes, she must use the XCOPY command instead of COPY. The XCOPY command provides exit codes that can incorporate ERRORLEVEL checks and provide explanations for each. (A user will not understand what an ERRORLEVEL 2 means.) You will have to use labels and GOTO statements. Print the contents of this new MOVEDIR.BAT file.

Case Study 3: The DOS Reference Card

In this case study, you continue creating the DOS reference card you began in Chapter 3. Several terms and DOS commands are introduced in this chapter and should be added to the reference card. Fill in the command, term, or key sequence that matches each description.

Description	Command/Term/Sequence	Type
A text file containing commands that DOS executes as though the commands were entered at the DOS prompt.	_____	Term
Holds the place for a parameter in one or more commands of a batch file so that you can provide the actual value.	_____	Term
A special batch file that DOS executes each time you boot the computer.	_____	Term

(continues)

Description	Command/Term/Sequence	Type
Enables you to insert into a batch file comments that describe the intent of an operation.	_____	Command
Allows the use of the same batch command for several files	_____	Command
Used to abort or terminate a batch file.	_____	Sequence
Jumps to the line following the specified label in a batch file.	_____	Command
Runs another batch file and returns to the original batch file.	_____	Command
Enables you to include a message from within a batch file.	_____	Command
Suppresses the display of the command line on-screen.	_____	Command
Allows conditional execution of a command within a batch file.	_____	Command

 # Challenge Problems

1. Batch files enable you to perform multiple commands easily. Replaceable parameters act as fill-in-the-blanks when a batch file executes. Here's the challenge. When writing a batch file that uses the COPY command, the files that are copied are echoed to the screen, and a `Files copied` message appears after the copy is complete. How can you keep the files from listing and the `Files copied` message from appearing on-screen?

2. Batch files can use the ECHO command to display messages that you write. This capability is extremely useful when checking error-level codes. A good batch file will have only a single

line of text, usually displayed near the center of the screen, to indicate to the user what the batch file is doing. Having a single message on-screen enables the user to notice an error message quickly. A computer screen has 24 rows and 80 columns. How can you insert blank lines in a batch file so that a message will be displayed at line 12?

Answers to Odd-Numbered Questions

Key Term Matching Questions

1.	d	11.	g
3.	i	13.	c
5.	a	15.	j
7.	h	17.	r
9.	e	19.	k

Multiple-Choice Questions

1.	e	7.	d
3.	b	9.	d
5.	e		

True/False Questions

1.	T	7.	F
3.	T	9.	F
5.	F		

Data Files to Active Learning

Exercise	Beginning Name	Ending Name
Directed Exercise		
1	AUTOEXEC.BAT	AUTOEXEC.BAT
2	EASY.BAT	EASY.BAT
3	LOOP.BAT	LOOP.BAT
4	AUTOEXEC.BAT AUTOEXEC.OLD	AUTOEXEC.OLD AUTOEXEC.BAT
5	DCOPY.BAT	DCOPY.BAT

Mastering DOSKEY and Macros

Chapter Summary

Chapter 17 covers an alternative to batch files. You can use the DOSKEY program to create simple macros that quickly accomplish a series of tasks. This chapter shows how to use DOSKEY to make entering DOS commands easier and faster, as well as how to record commonly used commands as macros. DOSKEY remembers the commands you type at the DOS prompt, enabling you to use these commands again without retyping them. The chapter covers the following key points:

- DOSKEY enables you to redisplay a command that you issued earlier during the current DOS session.

- DOSKEY macros are stored in memory (RAM).

- Macros can contain multiple DOS commands, but are limited to 127 characters.

- The GOTO command is not available in macros.

Chapter Outline

I. Using DOSKEY

    A. Loading DOSKEY
    B. Editing the Command Line
    C. Reusing Commands

II. Creating and Using Macros

    A. Creating Macros
    B. Running Macros
    C. Deleting Macros

Active Learning

Key Term Matching

Match the following key terms with the definitions listed after them.

_____ 1. End

_____ 2. F5

_____ 3. Alt-F10

_____ 4. Home

_____ 5. Alt-F7

_____ 6. /BUFSIZE

_____ 7. gg

_____ 8. /INSERT

_____ 9. F6

_____10. Memory-resident

_____11. /OVERSTRIKE

_____12. F8

_____13. DOSKEY

_____14. Escape

_____15. /MACROS

_____16. $G

_____17. /HISTORY

_____18. Macro

_____19. PgUp

_____20. F2

Definitions

a. This DOSKEY option sets the size of the command buffer.

b. A series of commands stored in memory and assigned to a new command name to take the place of several DOS commands.

c. Pressing this key produces an end-of-file marker (^Z) when you copy from the console to a disk file.

d. Pressing this clears all macro definitions.

e. A program that allows you to edit and reuse DOS commands without retyping them.

f. This DOSKEY option displays a list of the currently defined DOSKEY macros.

g. Pressing this key copies all characters from the preceding command line up to, but not including, the next character you type.

17

h. This DOSKEY command-line editing key moves the cursor to the left end of the command line.

i. A program that remains in memory once invoked.

j. This DOSKEY option displays the contents of the command-history buffer.

k. This DOSKEY command-line editing key moves the cursor to the space after the last character in the command line.

l. Used in a macro to redirect and append output.

m. Pressing this displays the earliest command issued that is still stored in the DOSKEY command buffer.

n. This DOSKEY command-line editing key erases the command line.

o. This DOSKEY option instructs DOS to insert new text in place of existing text at the cursor position.

p. Clears the command-history buffer.

q. Used in a macro to redirect output.

r. Pressing this searches for the command that most closely matches the characters typed at the command line.

s. This DOSKEY option instructs DOS to insert new text into the existing text at the cursor position.

t. Pressing this key moves the current line into the buffer but prevents DOS from executing the line.

Multiple-Choice Questions

_____ 1. DOSKEY occupies only about _____ of memory.

      a. 8K
      b. 4K
      c. 512 bytes
      d. 1K
      e. 32K

_____ 2. The most convenient way to load DOSKEY is to

      a. type it at the command line.
      b. include it in the CONFIG.SYS file.
      c. include it in the AUTOEXEC.BAT file.
      d. include it in the DOS.INI file.
      e. include it in the ANSI.SYS file.

_____ 3. The DOSKEY option to display a list of the currently defined macros is:

      a. /LIST
      b. /HISTORY
      c. /REINSTALL
      d. /MACROS
      e. There is no such DOSKEY option.

_____ 4. Pressing the _____ key copies one character from the preceding command line.

      a. F1
      b. F2
      c. right arrow
      d. F3
      e. both a and b

_____ 5. The _____ key erases the command line.

      a. Ins
      b. Escape
      c. Ctrl-left arrow
      d. End
      e. Ctrl-right arrow

True/False Questions

____ 1. Using the Ctrl-left arrow key combination with DOSKEY moves the cursor one character to the left.

____ 2. To view the entire list of commands currently stored in the command-history buffer, press F7.

____ 3. DOS will not allow you to use a macro name that is the same as an existing DOS command because it would effectively replace the DOS command with the macro.

____ 4. When viewing the commands contained in the command-history buffer, the most recent command issued is number 1.

____ 5. The first DOSKEY command in AUTOEXEC.BAT loads the program as memory-resident, even if the command also is defining a macro.

17

▶ Directed Exercises

Exercise 1: Loading DOSKEY

In this exercise, you practice loading the DOSKEY command with several of its options. This exercise assumes that DOSKEY is *not* loaded in the AUTOEXEC.BAT file. Follow these steps:

1. Print a report on the programs in memory by typing **mem /c > prn** and pressing **Enter**.

2. Review the printed list to see if DOSKEY is shown on the list. If it is, use the DOS EDIT command to remove the command from the AUTOEXEC.BAT file and reboot your computer. Repeat step 1.

3. Enter the DOSKEY command into memory by typing **doskey** at the DOS prompt and pressing **Enter**. What message was displayed on-screen by this command?

4. Print a second report on the programs in memory by typing **mem /c > prn** and pressing **Enter**.

5. Compare the new printed list to the first list obtained in step 1.

   a. Does the DOSKEY command appear?

   b. How much memory does it take for the DOSKEY command?

6. Display the contents of the command-history buffer by typing **doskey /history** and pressing **Enter**. How many commands are in the command-history buffer?

7. Enter several DOS commands as shown below:

   a. **chkdsk**

   b. **dir c:\dos /p/w**

   c. **prompt pg**

   d. **type c:\autoexec.bat**

   e. **chkdsk c: /v**

8. Display the contents of the command-history buffer again by typing **doskey /history** and pressing **Enter**.

   a. Compare the results to what you received in step 6.

   b. How many commands are in the command-history buffer now?

9. Press the up-arrow key as many times as necessary to repeat the command TYPE C:\AUTOEXEC.BAT on the command line.

   a. How many times did you need to press the up-arrow key?

   b. Edit the command to read **type c:\config.sys**.

10. Display the contents of the command-history buffer again by typing **doskey /history** and pressing **Enter**.

   a. Compare the results to what you received in steps 6 and 8.

   b. How many commands are in the command-history buffer now?

   c. How many TYPE commands appear?

11. Press **Alt-F7** and press **Enter**, and then display the contents of the command-history buffer again by typing **doskey /history** and pressing **Enter**.

    a. Compare the results to what you received in previous steps.

    b. How many commands are in the command-history buffer now?

Exercise 2: Creating and Using Macros

In this exercise, you create your own DOS commands, referred to as *macros*. A macro is similar to a batch file but is contained in memory rather than on disk and can contain one or more DOS commands up to a maximum of 127 characters. This exercise assumes that Drive B: is a 3 1/2-inch, high-density floppy disk drive. Follow these steps:

1. Create a macro that will perform a quick format on either high-density or double-density floppy disks in Drive B: by typing **doskey fb=format b: /q ?f:$*** and then pressing **Enter**.

2. Create a second macro that will copy all files in the \DOS subdirectory on Drive C: ending with the file extension SYS to the newly formatted floppy disk in Drive B:. Create the macro by typing **doskey cp=copy c:\dos*.sys b:** and then pressing **Enter**.

3. Confirm that DOSKEY has stored the macros you defined by typing **doskey /macros** and pressing **Enter.**

4. Test the first macro by placing an unformatted 3 1/2-inch, double-density disk in Drive A: (or one that does not contain data you want to save) and typing **fb 720** then pressing **Enter**. *Note:* If you have a high-density disk, enter **fb 1.44** instead.

5. Test the second macro by typing **cp** and then pressing **Enter**.

6. Create a file named MACROS.BAT on your data disk in the CH17 subdirectory on Drive A: by typing the following command: **doskey /macros > a:\ch17\macros.bat.**

Continuing Problems

Refer to the complete description of the case studies in Chapter 3.

Case Study 1: Burke's Musical Instruments

Because Burke's Musical Instruments has been using a lot of tempo-rary employees lately, Debbie Burke has decided to create a series of macros to make the repeated commands more efficient. She has developed five macros that she wants the temporary employees to use every time. How can she make sure that they are available each time the computer is turned on?

Case Study 2: Medical Offices of Colby, Odenthal, Bravo & Kim

Dr. Christina Colby has returned from a long vacation in the Baha-mas and plans to continue her training sessions with Dr. Su-Jin Kim and other employees. She heard about the DOSKEY option from a fellow tourist, but he wasn't able to fully explain how she might use this command to make her training sessions easier. Can you think of how DOSKEY might facilitate training people to learn DOS commands?

Case Study 3: The DOS Reference Card

In this case study, you continue creating the DOS reference card you began in Chapter 3. Several terms and DOS commands are introduced in this chapter and should be added to the reference card. Fill in the command, term, or key sequence that matches each description.

Description	Command/Term/Sequence	Type
A new command that can take the place of several commands.	_____	Term
A memory-resident command that enables you to create new commands or edit and reuse DOS commands without retyping.	_____	Command

Answers to Odd-Numbered Questions

Key Term Matching Questions

1. k   11. o

3. d   13. e

5. p   15. f

7. l   17. j

9. c   19. m

Multiple-Choice Questions

1. b

3. d

5. b

True/False Questions

1. F

3. F

5. T

Data Files to Active Learning

Exercise	Beginning Name	Ending Name
Directed Exercise		
2	MACROS.BAT	MACROS.BAT

Configuring Your Computer

Chapter Summary

Chapter 18 is a comprehensive collection of DOS commands and directives that can help you get the best performance from your PC. In this chapter, you learn to use Microsoft MemMaker, a utility that automatically, and optimally, configures the way your PC uses RAM. It also covers how to set up CONFIG.SYS and AUTOEXEC.BAT files to provide the best overall system configuration.

This chapter presents the following important points:

- DOS can alter your system's configuration through instructions in the CONFIG.SYS and AUTOEXEC.BAT files.

- The CONFIG.SYS file must be in the root directory of the boot disk. When you alter CONFIG.SYS, configuration changes do not occur until DOS is rebooted.

- Disk buffers make DOS work faster by placing requested information in RAM.

- DOS provides several memory management features that can free significant portions of conventional memory as well as speed the operation of your system.

- The FILES command sets the number of files DOS can open at any one time.

- The LASTDRIVE command specifies the last disk drive letter you want to use in your system.

- You can tell DOS when to look for the Ctrl-Break key sequence.

Chapter Outline

I. Getting the Most from Your Computer Resources

II. Understanding Device Drivers

III. Optimizing Your Computer's Memory

    A. Using Extended Memory and HIMEM.SYS
    B. Loading DOS into High Memory
    C. Using Expanded Memory and EMM386.EXE
    D. Loading Device Drivers and TSRs into Upper Memory
    E. Displaying the Amount of Free and Used Memory
    F. Configuring Memory with MemMaker

IV. Increasing Hard Disk Performance

V. Fine-Tuning Your Computer with CONFIG.SYS and AUTOEXEC.BAT

    A. Accessing Files through FCBS
    B. Using the FILES Command
    C. Using LASTDRIVE to Change the Number of Disk Drives
    D. Using the SHELL Command
    E. Using the INSTALL Command
    F. Using the REM Command
    G. Using the SWITCHES Command
    H. Telling DOS When to Break
    I. Using the DOS Pretender Commands
    J. Using Other Device Control Commands

Active Learning

Key Term Matching

Match the following key terms with the definitions listed after them.

_____ 1. EMM386.EXE   _____ 11. DISPLAY.SYS

_____ 2. LASTDRIVE   _____ 12. FILES

_____ 3. High Memory Area (HMA)   _____ 13. BUFFERS

_____ 4. REM   _____ 14. FILES

_____ 5. CONFIG.SYS   _____ 15. SHELL

_____ 6. AUTOEXEC.BAT   _____ 16. BREAK

_____ 7. INSTALL   _____ 17. Buffer

_____ 8. Device driver   _____ 18. SWITCHES

_____ 9. RAMDRIVE.SYS   _____ 19. HIMEM.SYS

_____ 10. MOUSE.COM   _____ 20. Upper Memory Area (UMA)

18

Definitions

a. Informs DOS that the command interpreter is in a directory other than the boot disk's root directory.

b. A category of "plug-in modules" that give DOS the information needed to access various types of hardware devices.

c. This consists of the 384K of memory above 640K up to 1M and is divided into many different sized blocks called upper memory blocks (UMBs).

d. This configuration command determines the number of files that can be open at one time during a DOS session.

e. Device drivers are loaded with this.

f. This DOS device driver enables applications to use extended memory as though it were expanded memory.

g. Tells DOS when to look for a Ctrl-C key sequence.

h. This device driver uses a portion of random-access memory to simulate a hard disk.

i. This command enables you to insert remarks into your CONFIG.SYS file.

j. This device driver manages extended memory.

k. Tells DOS how much memory to reserve for file transfers.

l. This configuration command informs DOS of the maximum number of disk drives on your system.

m. This device driver provides support for a Microsoft mouse.

n. One use of this command is to turn off the enhanced keyboard functions.

o. This can load applications and execute DOS commands.

p. If you don't specify this command with a value larger than 8, you only have three file handles for your programs.

q. This is a single block of memory essentially consisting of the first 64K of extended memory.

r. This configuration command enables you to load memory-resident programs from within CONFIG.SYS.

s. This device driver provides support for code-page switching to the screen.

t. An area of RAM set aside for temporary storage of data being transferred between a disk and an applications program.

Multiple-Choice Questions

_____ 1. Which of the following device drivers sets parameters for physical and logical disk drives?

      a. DISPLAY.SYS
      b. HIMEM.SYS
      c. DRIVER.SYS
      d. CHKSTATE.SYS
      e. SSTOR.SYS

____ 2. The single block of memory essentially consisting of the first 64K of extended memory is known as

      a. upper memory area (UMA).
      b. high memory area (HMA).
      c. upper memory blocks (UMB).
      d. extended memory blocks (XMS).
      e. expanded memory blocks (EMS).

____ 3. By loading the operating system into high memory, DOS 6.2 can free about ____ of conventional memory.

      a. 47K
      b. 62K
      c. 14K
      d. 386K
      e. 29K

____ 4. To load DOS into the high memory area your ____ file should contain the command ____.

      a. AUTOEXEC.BAT; DOS=HIGH,UMB
      b. CONFIG.SYS; DOS=HIGH,HMA
      c. HIMEM.SYS; DOS=HIGH,HMA
      d. CONFIG.SYS; DOS=HIGH,UMB
      e. ANSI.SYS; DOS=HIGH,UMB

18

____ 5. An easy way to run MemMaker is to use the ____ switch.

      a. /CUSTOM
      b. /EXPRESS
      c. /BATCH
      d. /AUTO
      e. /DEFAULT

____ 6. If you have a hard disk of 80M to 119M, the number of buffers you should allocate is

      a. 50.
      b. 30.
      c. 10.
      d. 20.
      e. 40.

____ 7. By default, the number of files that DOS allows to be open at one time during a session is

    a. 8.
    b. 10.
    c. 16.
    d. 24.
    e. 12.

____ 8. Using the ____ switch with the SWITCHES configuration command tells DOS to ignore F5 or F8 during boot.

    a. /W
    b. /N
    c. /F
    d. /K
    e. /S

____ 9. The ____ driver uses a portion of random-access memory to simulate a hard disk.

    a. SSTOR.SYS
    b. POWER.EXE
    c. DRIVER.SYS
    d. RAMDRIVE.SYS
    e. HIMEM.SYS

____ 10. Which of the following is not a device driver?

    a. PRINTER.SYS
    b. CHKSTATE.SYS
    c. ANSI.SYS
    d. HIMEM.SYS
    e. COUNTRY.SYS

True/False Questions

____ 1. The High Memory Area (HMA) consists of 384K of memory above 640K up to 1M and is divided into many different sized blocks.

____ 2. The DOS Device driver EMM386.EXE enables applications to use extended memory as though it were expanded memory.

_____ 3. Most current versions of commercial software support the HMA specification for addressing extended memory.

_____ 4. KEYBOARD.SYS is not a device driver and cannot be used in a CONFIG.SYS file.

_____ 5. To load device drivers or memory-resident programs (TSRs) into upper memory, your computer must have HIMEM.SYS loaded as a device driver.

_____ 6. BREAK=OFF disables the break key, and BREAK=ON enables it.

_____ 7. If you do not use the LASTDRIVE command, DOS assumes that the last disk drive on your system is one more than the number of physical drives and RAM disks you are using.

_____ 8. If used incorrectly, the SHELL command can lock up your system.

_____ 9. The maximum number of files that DOS will allow to be open at one time during a DOS session is 255.

_____ 10. Computers usually cannot access instructions from RAM as fast as they can access instructions from ROM.

18

▶ Directed Exercises

Exercise 1: Identifying Device Drivers

This exercise is designed to give you practice identifying the purpose of various device drivers. Give a brief description for each of the following device drivers:

1. ANSI.SYS

2. DISPLAY.SYS

3. DRIVER.SYS

4. EGA.SYS

5. EMM386.EXE

6. HIMEM.SYS

7. INTERLNK.EXE

8. PRINTER.SYS

9. RAMDRIVE.SYS

10. SETVER.EXE

Exercise 2: Working with CONFIG.SYS

In this exercise, you practice creating a CONFIG.SYS file that loads DOS into upper memory. You then discover how this change affects conventional memory. This exercise assumes that you are using a computer with a hard drive designated as Drive C: and that an existing CONFIG.SYS file is in the root directory of Drive C:. It also assumes that you have a printer powered on and connected to your computer. Follow these steps:

1. Print the contents of CONFIG.SYS and also copy it to a file named CONFIG.TST (just in case something accidentally gets deleted or changed).

2. Rename the existing CONFIG.SYS file to a new file called CONFIG.OLD. You should have two files, CONFIG.TST and CONFIG.OLD, containing the same contents.

3. Copy the AUTOEXEC.BAT file to a file named AUTOEXEC.TST and rename the existing AUTOEXEC.BAT file **AUTOEXEC.BAR** so that it will not execute when you reboot the computer.

4. Use the DOS Editor to create a new CONFIG.SYS file containing only the following lines of text:

   FILES = 30

   BUFFERS = 15

5. Save the file and reboot your computer to use the modified CONFIG.SYS file.

6. At the DOS system prompt, type **mem /c** and press **Enter** to bring up a table containing conventional memory information on the screen.

7. Print the screen contents by using PrintScreen so that you can examine the report.

8. Find the name MSDOS, and record the amount or size being used by MSDOS.

    a. Was this size approximately 57K?

    b. Did COMMAND require approximately 4.6K of memory?

    c. Write down the number of bytes available to programs.

9. Edit the CONFIG.SYS file and add the following lines of text:

    DEVICE=C:\DOS\HIMEM.SYS

    DOS=HIGH

10. Save and print the file, and then reboot your computer again.

11. At the DOS command line, type **mem /c** once again and press **Enter**.

12. Print the screen contents using PrintScreen and compare it to the previous report.

    a. What are the size differences between what was shown previously for MSDOS and COMMAND?

    b. How much more memory has been regained by loading DOS into upper memory?

13. If you are not immediately continuing on to exercise 3, restore the original CONFIG.SYS and AUTOEXEC.BAT files.

18

Exercise 3: Loading TSRs from CONFIG.SYS

This exercise is designed to give you practice loading a Terminate-and-Stay-Resident program (TSR) into upper memory and conventional memory. You will compare loading a TSR from CONFIG.SYS to loading it with AUTOEXEC.BAT or from the DOS system prompt. This exercise assumes that you have completed exercises 1 and 2 immediately before starting exercise 3. DOSKEY is the TSR that will be used in this exercise. Follow these steps:

1. Edit the CONFIG.SYS file to install the DOSKEY program. The following line of text should be added to the CONFIG.SYS file:

    INSTALL=C:\DOS\DOSKEY.COM

2. Reboot your computer.

    a. Is the DOSKEY program available?

    b. How did you check to see whether DOSKEY was available?

3. Edit the CONFIG.SYS file, and remove the line where you installed the DOSKEY program.

4. At the DOS command line, type **doskey** and press **Enter**. Is DOSKEY available?

5. Edit the AUTOEXEC.BAT file and add the following line of text:

    c:\dos\doskey

6. Save the file, and reboot your computer.

    a. Is DOSKEY available?

    b. How did you check to see whether DOSKEY was available?

7. Edit the AUTOEXEC.BAT file, and modify the previously entered line to read

    loadhigh c:\dos\doskey

8. Save the file again and reboot your computer once more.

    a. How did adding LOADHIGH effect DOSKEY?

    b. Does the DOSKEY program work?

    c. Which way is better when loading a TSR or does it matter?

9. Restore the original CONFIG.SYS and AUTOEXEC.BAT files.

Exercise 4: Configuring Memory with Memmaker

This exercise is designed to give you practice configuring memory with the DOS program MemMaker. MemMaker sorts device drivers and TSRs that you load in memory to see the optimum loading order, then updates your CONFIG.SYS and AUTOEXEC.BAT files. This exercise assumes that you are using a computer with a hard disk designated as Drive C: and that both the CONFIG.SYS and AUTOEXEC.BAT files are in the root directory of Drive C:. It also assumes that you have a printer powered on and connected to your computer. Follow these steps:

1. Before beginning to use MemMaker, examine your CONFIG.SYS file to make sure that it has the line DOS=HIGH in it. If it does not, edit the file to put this line in CONFIG.SYS and reboot the computer.

2. Print a copy of both the CONFIG.SYS and AUTOEXEC.BAT files.

3. At the DOS prompt, type **memmaker** and press **Enter**.

4. MemMaker asks whether you want to continue; press **Enter** to continue.

5. At the next prompt, press **Enter** to select an Express setup.

6. MemMaker asks whether you intend to use EMS (expanded) memory. Most systems do not use EMS memory so select N and press **Enter**.

7. Next, MemMaker will ask to reboot the computer.

   a. Press **Enter**. MemMaker reboots your computer.

   b. If it does not start correctly, turn it off and back on to reboot it manually.

8. When your computer reboots, MemMaker calculates the optimal configuration for your computer then asks to reboot again. Press **Enter** so that MemMaker can reboot a second time.

9. During this reboot, the computer executes the CONFIG.SYS and AUTOEXEC.BAT files that MemMaker creates.

   a. When the computer boots, be sure to watch carefully for any errors produced by the device drivers and programs loaded from your new CONFIG.SYS and AUTOEXEC.BAT files.

   b. MemMaker will ask whether you saw any errors during boot.

   c. If your computer booted without errors, press **Enter**.

10. MemMaker displays a table showing how the changes affected your available memory. Print a copy of this report by using PrintScreen.

11. Press **Enter** to exit MemMaker and return to the DOS prompt.

12. Print a copy of the new AUTOEXEC.BAT and CONFIG.SYS files and compare them to the original copies.

18

Continuing Problems

Refer to the complete description of the case studies in Chapter 3.

Case Study 1: Burke's Musical Instruments

Debbie decided to purchase a mouse for her computer system. She quickly opened the box, attached the mouse to the system, and copied the software to the hard disk. She started her computer and executed an application that uses a mouse. But to her surprise, the mouse didn't work. In her haste, she had torn up and thrown away the box that contained the instructions.

Issa decided to help Debbie and looked at the files that she copied onto the hard drive. There was only one file called MOUSE.SYS, but Issa knows that you cannot execute a SYS file. What is this file for, and how can Debbie and Issa get the computer to recognize the mouse?

Case Study 2: Medical Offices of Colby, Odenthal, Bravo & Kim

Firman Hartono is working on a project that involves database files containing large amounts of information. Using a database provides the flexibility to arrange the data on key fields. Firman performs a Sort operation to arrange the information in alphabetical order. This process takes approximately two to three hours. The database file isn't large, but it takes a long time to sort. How could Firman speed this sorting problem without changing any information in the database?

Case Study 3: The DOS Reference Card

In this case study, you continue creating the DOS reference card you began in Chapter 3. Several terms and DOS commands are introduced in this chapter and should be added to the reference card. Fill in the command, term, or key sequence that matches each description.

Description	Command/Term/Sequence	Type
The portion of RAM that is above 1,024K.		Term
The first 64K of extended memory.		Term
An area of memory between 640K and 1M.		Term
The portion of RAM that is 640K and less.		Term
A special program file that DOS loads through the CONFIG.SYS file.		Term
Displays the amount of used and unused memory allocated in open memory areas and in all programs currently in the system.		Command
Sets the number of file buffers DOS reserves for transferring information to and from the disk.		Command
Loads a driver that enables a particular device to be used with your system.		Command
Used to load a memory-resident program into upper memory.		Command
Loads a device driver into an upper memory block.		Command
Enables DOS to report specific version numbers to different programs for compatibility with DOS 5.		Command
Sets the number of files that can be opened at one time.		Command

18

(continues)

Description	Command/Term/Sequence	Type
Determines whether DOS is loaded into high memory area and whether upper memory blocks are allocated. _____		Command
Manages extended memory. _____		Driver

Challenge Problems

1. Nick Samia is having a problem with his computer. The company just upgraded all the computers with the latest version of the word processing package they use. When Nick tried to run the program, a message appeared indicating that FILES must equal 30 or more before the program will start. Explain what Nick should do to fix this problem and how you determined what needed fixing.

2. The computer that Dawn Castiglione uses at work contains a large hard disk. Her boss asked her to write a technical report on the uses of computers within their organization. Dawn remembered that she wrote a similar report two months ago called CMP_TECH.RPT and decides that modifying this file would be much easier than creating a new file. The only problem is that she doesn't remember where she stored the file on the hard disk. Which DOS command should Dawn use, and with which parameters and/or switches, to find this file?

Answers to Odd-Numbered Questions

Key Term Matching Questions

1.	f	11.	s
3.	q	13.	k
5.	e	15.	a
7.	r	17.	t
9.	h	19.	j

Multiple-Choice Questions

1.	c	7.	a
3.	a	9.	d
5.	c		

True/False Questions

1.	F	7.	T
3.	F	9.	T
5.	T		

18

Getting the Most from Your Hard Drive

Chapter Summary

Chapter 19 describes how to keep a hard disk at its most efficient level. This chapter describes SMARTDrive, a disk cache that increases the speed of accessing data on the hard disk. You also learn about Microsoft Defrag, a utility that keeps files in proper order, and DoubleSpace, the DOS program that virtually doubles the space available for information storage on the disk drives.

In Chapter 19, you discover the utility programs that DOS provides to enable you to use your hard disk most efficiently. The chapter covers the following important points:

- You can increase the effective speed with which you can access data on your hard disk by creating a disk cache with SMARTDrive.

- A RAM disk, created with RAMDRIVE, can help improve program speed for programs using many temporary files.

- Defragmenting your disk regularly with DEFRAG improves disk access and loading times.

- You can increase the amount of space available by using disk compression with DoubleSpace.

Chapter Outline

I. Getting the Most Speed from Your Hard Drive

    A. Using a Disk Cache (SMARTDrive)
    B. Using FASTOPEN
    C. Using a RAM Disk
    D. Defragmenting Your Disk

II. Getting the Most Space from Your Hard Disk

III. Freeing Up Disk Space

    A. Deleting Unnecessary Files
    B. Using File Compression
    C. Archiving Files

IV. Understanding DoubleSpace

    A. Installing DoubleSpace
    B. Controlling the Operation of DoubleSpace
    C. Displaying Compressed Drive Information
    D. Changing the Size of a Compressed Drive
    E. Changing the Compression Ratio
    F. Formatting a Compressed Drive
    G. Deleting a Compressed Drive
    H. Creating a New Uncompressed Drive
    I. Using Other DoubleSpace Features

Active Learning

Key Term Matching

Match the following key terms with the definitions listed after them.

____	1. SMARTDRV	____	11. RAM disk
____	2. WAV	____	12. Compression
____	3. DoubleSpace	____	13. GIF
____	4. Compression ratio	____	14. Cache
____	5. /S:D	____	15. /S:S
____	6. SCANFIX	____	16. DRIVER.SYS
____	7. Fragmentation	____	17. DEFRAG
____	8. Flushing	____	18. CONFIG.SYS
____	9. AUTOEXEC.BAT	____	19. FASTOPEN
____	10. /S:N	____	20. RAMDRIVE.SYS

Definitions

a. The condition where data within a single file may reside in chunks throughout the disk.

b. A file extension given to certain graphics files.

c. The disk-caching program that comes with DOS.

d. The file used to load RAMDRIVE.SYS.

e. A switch used with DEFRAG to sort entries within each directory by name.

f. A term that refers to the size of compressed data as compared to the size of the same data in its uncompressed state.

g. The RAM disk driver that comes with DOS.

h. This utility enables DOS to compress data automatically when you store the data on disk and to uncompress the data when you use it.

19

i. This term refers to the allocation of some of your memory for temporary data storage on disk.

j. A program similar to CHKDSK but intended to be used on compressed disks.

k. If this driver is loaded after RAMDRIVE.SYS, then the RAM disk may be named D, and this disk one letter higher.

l. A file extension given to certain sound files.

m. The file used to start SMARTDrive.

n. An executable program that caches hard drive directory information, holding in memory the locations of frequently used files and directories.

o. A switch used with DEFRAG to sort entries within each directory by date.

p. A DOS utility that moves all the data to the beginning of the disk and stores each file's data in the same place.

q. The term used for squeezing a file's data into a smaller space by converting the data to a kind of shorthand notation.

r. An operation that tells SMARTDrive that no more data will be written to disk and instructs it to finish writing whatever data it has accumulated.

s. This virtual disk is extremely fast compared with a real disk drive but its contents disappear when you turn off or reboot your computer.

t. A switch used with DEFRAG to sort entries within each directory by size.

Multiple-Choice Questions

_____ 1. The disk-caching program that comes with DOS is named:

    a. CACHE.EXE
    b. CACHE.COM
    c. SMARTDRV.EXE
    d. SMARTDRV.EXE
    e. DBLSPACE.EXE

____ 2. The total number of directory entries or fragmented entries FASTOPEN can handle is

    a. 16.
    b. 999.
    c. 200.
    d. 256.
    e. 24.

____ 3. The RAM disk driver that comes with DOS is loaded as a device driver in:

    a. RAMDRIVE.SYS
    b. CONFIG.SYS
    c. AUTOEXEC.BAT
    d. Windows
    e. the DOS system prompt

____ 4. If you don't specify any drive letters in your SMARTDRV command, ____ are read-cached but not write-cached, and ____ are read-cached and write-cached.

    a. CD-ROM drives; hard disk drives
    b. floppy disk drives; CD-ROM drives
    c. CD-ROM drives; floppy disk drives
    d. hard disk drives; floppy disk drives
    e. floppy disk drives; hard disk drives

____ 5. The default size of a RAM disk is

    a. 64KB.
    b. 1MB.
    c. 640KB.
    d. 256KB.
    e. 128KB.

19

____ 6. Which of the following is not a sort option available in DEFRAG?

    a. unsorted
    b. name
    c. size
    d. directory
    e. extension

_____ 7. Which of the following statements is not true about a drive compressed with DoubleSpace?

    a. You cannot unformat a compressed drive.

    b. You can read a compressed drive only if the DoubleSpace driver is loaded.

    c. DoubleSpace must perform extra work to compress and uncompress data each time you access your disk.

    d. Some graphic files (such as TIF files) are already compressed and do not benefit from DoubleSpace.

    e. When you apply compression to a drive, DoubleSpace makes the drive appear as though it were two drives with two distinct drive letters.

_____ 8. The program used to verify the integrity of a compressed volume is:

    a. CHKDSK

    b. SCAN

    c. SCANDSK

    d. CHKSYS

    e. CHKVOL

_____ 9. Which of the following would not be expected to speed up the performance of your computer?

    a. DBLSPACE

    b. RAMDRIVE

    c. DEFRAG

    d. SMARTDrive

    e. All of these answers will speed up your computer performance.

_____10. Which of the following options prevents SMARTDrive from loading into your upper-memory area (UMA)?

    a. /C

    b. /B

    c. /Q

    d. /N

    e. /L

True/False Questions

___ 1. You can use FASTOPEN with either floppy disk drives or hard disk drives.

___ 2. You may not want to use read-caching in an area with unreliable electrical power because of the risk of data loss.

___ 3. A RAM disk is used as any other disk drive except that the contents of the RAM disk disappear when you turn off or reboot your computer.

___ 4. Although you can load FASTOPEN as part of your regular configuration through CONFIG.SYS or AUTOEXEC.BAT, it can also be loaded from the DOS system prompt or through Windows Program Manager.

___ 5. Disk fragmentation is not only almost inevitable, it tends to increase the longer you use your disk.

___ 6. One of the recommended methods of freeing disk space is to delete files you no longer need.

___ 7. One of the files that should be compressed is the Windows swap file because it can take up a lot of unnecessary disk space.

___ 8. A disk-caching program like SMARTDrive remembers which sections of the disk you have used most frequently.

___ 9. You can use DEFRAG to determine whether your disk is fragmented.

___ 10. The more fragmented your disk, the more slowly your computer runs.

19

▶ Directed Exercises

Exercise 1: Disk-caching with SMARTDrive

This exercise gives you experience installing and using the DOS disk-caching program, SMARTDrive. You will examine memory allocations before and after SMARTDrive installation. This exercise assumes that you are using a computer with a hard drive designated as Drive C: and a floppy disk drive designated as Drive A:. It also assumes that there is a subdirectory on Drive C: called \DOS and that the AUTOEXEC.BAT file is in the root directory of Drive C:. To successfully complete the entire exercise, you will also need a powered-on printer connected to your computer. Follow these steps:

1. Before beginning, make the root directory of Drive C: your default by typing **C:** and pressing **Enter**, then typing **cd ** and pressing **Enter** again.

2. Examine your AUTOEXEC.BAT file to see whether SMARTDRV is already included in that file by entering **type autoexec.bat** and pressing **Enter**. If SMARTDRV is not included, go to step 3.

   a. If SMARTDRV is included in AUTOEXEC.BAT, use the DOS Editor to edit the file and place the letters **rem** at the beginning of the line containing the SMARTDRV command.

   b. Next, reboot your computer without the SMARTDRV statement in the AUTOEXEC.BAT file by pressing **Ctrl-Alt-Del**.

3. When you return to the DOS prompt, type **mem /p >prn** to print the detailed memory report.

4. Type **smartdrv /s** and press **Enter**. Print the response shown on-screen.

5. Type **smartdrv** and press **Enter**.

6. Type **mem /p >prn** again; print the second report and compare it to the previous report. Was there any difference?

7. Type **smartdrv /s** again and press **Enter**.

   a. Print the screen's response.

   b. How does it compare to the previous response?

8. Type **smartdrv c+ | a+** and press **Enter**, and then type **smartdrv /s** and press **Enter** again.

   a. Print the screen's response again.

   b. How does it compare to the previous responses?

9. Reboot the computer again by pressing **Ctrl-Alt-Del**.

10. This time prevent SMARTDRV from loading into your upper-memory area by typing **smartdrv /l** and pressing **Enter**. Make a note of the screen's response.

11. Type **mem /p >prn** again and press **Enter**. How does the report compare to the previous reports?

12. Type **smartdrv /s** again and press **Enter**.

   a. Print the screen's response.

   b. How does it compare to the previous responses?

13. Write a description for the following switches that can be used with SMARTDRV:

   a. +

   b. -

   c. /B:BufferSize

   d. /C

   e. /F

   f. /L

   g. /N

   h. /Q

   i. /U

   j. /X

14. Be sure to restore the AUTOEXEC.BAT file to its original condition before leaving the computer.

Exercise 2: Creating a RAM Disk

This exercise gives you experience creating a RAM disk by using the RAM disk driver that comes with DOS, RAMDRIVE.SYS. You examine memory allocations before and after creating the RAM disk. This exercise assumes that you are using a computer with a hard drive designated as Drive C:. It also assumes that there is a subdirectory on Drive C: called \DOS and that the CONFIG.SYS file is in the root directory of Drive C:. To successfully complete the entire exercise, you also will need a powered-on printer connected to your computer. Follow these steps:

   1. Before beginning, make the root directory of Drive C: your default by typing **c:** and pressing **Enter**, and then type **cd ** and press **Enter** again.

19

2. Examine your CONFIG.SYS file to see if RAMDRIVE.SYS is already included in that file by entering **type ramdrive.sys** and pressing **Enter**. If RAMDDRIVE.SYS is not included, go to step 3.

     a. If RAMDRIVE.SYS is included in CONFIG.SYS, copy CONFIG.SYS to another file called CONFIG.RAM by typing **copy config.sys config.ram** and pressing **Enter**.

     b. Use the DOS Editor to edit the CONFIG.SYS file. Delete the line referring to RAMDRIVE and save the file.

     c. Next, reboot your computer without the RAMDRIVE statement in the CONFIG.SYS file by pressing **Ctrl-Alt-Del**.

3. When you return to the DOS prompt, type **mem /p >prn** to print out the detailed memory report.

4. Use the DOS Editor to edit the CONFIG.SYS file by including the following line:

     device = ramdrive.sys

5. Reboot your computer with the RAMDRIVE statement in the CONFIG.SYS file by pressing **Ctrl-Alt-Del**.

6. When the computer is booted, type **mem /p >prn** again; print out the second report and compare it to the previous report. Was there any difference?

7. Edit the CONFIG.SYS file again by changing the new line you just entered to read **devicehigh = ramdrive.sys 1024 /e** and pressing **Enter**.

8. Reboot the computer again by pressing **Ctrl-Alt-Del**.

9. Type **mem /p >prn** again and press **Enter**. How does the report compare to the previous reports?

10. Restore the original CONFIG.SYS file by doing the following:

     a. Type **del config.sys** and press **Enter**.

     b. Type **ren config.ram config.sys** and press **Enter**.

Exercise 3: Using DEFRAG

This exercise gives you experience using DEFRAG, the defragmentation program that comes with DOS. This exercise assumes that you are using a computer with a hard drive designated as Drive C: and a floppy disk drive designated as Drive A:. To gain experience with this program, you first practice the exercise on the floppy disk in Drive A: and, *only with permission from your instructor*, perhaps then on Drive C:. To successfully complete the entire exercise, you also will need a powered-on printer connected to your computer.

1. At the DOS prompt, type **defrag** and press **Enter**.

2. When the DEFRAG disk selection dialog box appears, select Drive A:. You can select Drive A: either by using a mouse to click on the drive letter or by using the arrow key to move to the designation and then pressing **Enter**.

3. DEFRAG scans the selected drive and displays a map of its used and unused portion.

    a. Use the **PrintScreen** key to obtain a hard copy of this map.

    b. Study the legend at the bottom right corner of the screen to understand the symbols in the disk map.

4. If the disk is not fragmented, DEFRAG tells you that you don't need to perform any operation. In this case, you might want to repeat the above steps with another floppy disk until you find one that DEFRAG can optimize.

5. When you have the DEFRAG Optimize Menu, select About Defrag and read the information displayed about the DEFRAG program before continuing.

6. When you return to the menu, follow these steps:

    a. Select Optimization Method.

    b. Then select Full Optimization.

    c. Next select File Sort and sort the files by Name.

    d. Finally choose Begin Optimization to start the DEFRAG process.

7. You can repeat the process on other floppy disks in either Drive A: or Drive B:.

8. *Do this step only with instructor permission.* Repeat the above process for Drive C:, and compare the length of time for optimization to how long it took for the floppy drive to become optimized. ***Note:*** Do not attempt the DEFRAG process if you are using a network drive or if you are running Windows.

19

Continuing Problems

Refer to the complete description of the Case Studies in Chapter 3.

Case Study 1: Burke's Musical Instruments

Shinichi Murakami has really become quite expert using the computer at Burke's Musical Instruments. In fact, he has gotten so expert that he is constantly complaining that the computer is too slow. He remembers hearing that there are several ways to speed up the computer without having to upgrade the CPU. Make a list of things Shinichi could try that might improve the speed performance of the company's computer.

Case Study 2: Medical Offices Of Colby, Odenthal, Bravo & Kim

The medical office staff has noticed that the hard disk on the computer is almost full but the doctors do not want to purchase another computer or a larger hard disk at this time. Make a list of things they should do to maximize the use of the hard disk they have.

Case Study 3: The DOS Reference Card

In this case study, you continue creating the DOS reference card you began in Chapter 3. Several terms and DOS commands are introduced in this chapter and should be added to the reference card. Fill in the command, term, or key sequence that matches each description.

Description	Command/Term/Sequence	Type
When a file resides in noncontiguous chunks throughout the disk.	_____	Term
The DOS RAM disk driver.	_____	Command
Enables DOS to compress data automatically when you store it on a disk.	_____	Command
Squeezing a file's data into a smaller space.	_____	Term
Caches hard drive directory information, holding in memory the locations of frequently used files.	_____	Command
Extended memory disk cache that can increase performance of disk functions.	_____	Command
Defragments files on disk to optimize disk performance.	_____	Command

Answers to Odd-Numbered Questions

19

Key Term Matching Questions

1. c
3. h
5. o
7. a
9. m

11. s
13. b
15. t
17. p
19. n

Multiple-Choice Questions

1. c
3. b
5. a

7. d
9. a

True/False Questions

1. F
3. T
5. T

7. F
9. T

Understanding ANSI.SYS

Chapter Summary

Chapter 20 is the first of two chapters designed to top off your understanding of DOS by showing you how to control and program the screen and keyboard. You learn how to make DOS screens look colorful and controlled, how to reassign keys, control the cursor's position on-screen, display the date and time, and more.

The chapter covers the following key points:

- You communicate with ANSI.SYS by issuing Escape sequences.

- You cannot issue an Escape sequence from the command line.

- You can issue an Escape sequence in a batch file, a prompt command, and a text file that you TYPE to the display.

- You use MS-DOS EDIT to create the batch and text files for ANSI.SYS commands.

- You can change screen attributes and colors with the ANSI.SYS commands.

- You can change key definitions with the ANSI.SYS commands.

Chapter Outline

I. Installing ANSI.SYS

II. Using ANSI.SYS

    A. Issuing ANSI.SYS Codes in Batch Files
    B. Issuing ANSI.SYS Codes in Text Files
    C. Issuing ANSI.SYS Codes with the PROMPT Command

III. Controlling Your Screen with ANSI.SYS

    A. Cursor Movement
    B. Cursor Positioning
    C. Setting the Screen Mode
    D. Setting the Text Attributes
    E. Screen Control

IV. Customizing Your Keyboard with ANSI.SYS

Active Learning

Key Term Matching

Match the following key terms with the definitions listed after them.

_____ 1. Screen code 3

_____ 2. White background color

_____ 3. Screen Code 7

_____ 4. Hidden text

_____ 5. ^[[

_____ 6. Reverse video

_____ 7. ASCII character set

_____ 8. ANSI.SYS

_____ 9. Screen code 0

_____ 10. /X

_____ 11. Screen code 6

_____ 12. Blue background

_____ 13. CONFIG.SYS

_____ 14. /K

_____ 15. Normal display

_____ 16. [

_____ 17. ANSI Code 37

_____ 18. /R

_____ 19. Blinking text

_____ 20. ANSI Code 41

Definitions

a. The only way you can install the ANSI.SYS driver is to include it in this file.

b. Produced with ANSI character attribute code 7.

c. The ANSI code for a red background.

d. Enables you to remap extended keys if your are using a 101-key keyboard.

e. Produced with code 47.

f. All ANSI.SYS sequences begin with the Escape character followed by this.

g. A device driver that gives DOS additional control for the screen and keyboard devices beyond the control features built into the operating system.

h. Turns word wrap on and off.

i. Produced with ANSI character attribute code 5.

j. Treats 101-key keyboards as if they were 84-key keyboards, ignoring extended keys.

k. Provides the screen type of 80 x 25 characters, color.

l. A set of 256 codes to indicate specific characters.

m. Produced with ANSI character attribute code 0.

n. Some text editors display an ANSI sequence as this.

o. Slows screen scrolling for improved readability.

p. Produces the screen type of 40 x 25 characters, monochrome.

q. Produced with ANSI character attribute code 8.

r. Produces a white foreground.

s. The result of code 44.

t. Produces the screen type of 640 x 200 pixels, monochrome.

Multiple-Choice Questions

____ 1. The only way you can install the ANSI.SYS driver is

     a. to include it in your CONFIG.SYS file.
     b. put it in the AUTOEXEC.BAT file.
     c. execute it from the DOS system prompt.
     d. all of these answers
     e. none of these answers

____ 2. All ANSI.SYS sequences begin with the ____ character.

     a. [
     b. \
     c. ^
     d. Esc
     e. @

____ 3. The ANSI code ____ produces a red background.

     a. 37
     b. 41
     c. 44
     d. 39
     e. 43

____ 4. If you end an ANSI screen command with the uppercase letter ____, ANSI.SYS assumes that you want to move the cursor up a given number of lines on-screen.

     a. B
     b. U
     c. A
     d. D
     e. X

____ 5. The ANSI code for setting the default character attributes for normal display is

     a. 8.
     b. 4.
     c. 7.
     d. 1.
     e. 0.

True/False Questions

____ 1. Screen code 7 turns word wrap on and off.

____ 2. Using the proper ANSI code can create special text effects, such as underlined text, on any monitor.

____ 3. The ASCII character set is 254 codes to indicate specific characters.

____ 4. The ANSI.SYS keyboard-assignment Escape sequence contains the standard characters (Escape []) followed by a space, then the ASCII code, the scan code, or the key representation in quotation marks.

____ 5. A key assignment does not need to be a single character; you also can assign a text message to a keystroke.

▶ Directed Exercises

Exercise 1: Examining ANSI.SYS

In this exercise, you determine whether ANSI.SYS is currently being loaded in your computer's CONFIG.SYS file. The exercise assumes that you are using a computer with a hard disk designated as Drive C: and that a CONFIG.SYS file exists in the root directory of Drive C:. It also assumes that the default ANSI.SYS file is contained in a \DOS subdirectory on Drive C:. Follow these steps:

1. After booting your computer, make sure that you are in the root directory of Drive C:.

2. Use the TYPE command to view the contents of the CONFIG.SYS file.

    a. Do all of the lines appear on one screen? If not, use the |MORE filter to pause the display at the end of each screenful.

    b. Is a line containing ANSI.SYS shown in your CONFIG.SYS file?

3. Use the CD command to make the C:\DOS subdirectory the default.

20

4. Use the DIR command to determine if ANSI.SYS is present.

5. If the TYPE command is there, use it to view the contents of the ANSI.SYS file.

    a. What does it look like?

    b. Do you recognize any of the commands or does it appear to be "garbage" characters?

Exercise 2: Using ANSI.SYS Commands in a Batch File

In this exercise, you practice writing a batch file to set up formatting for a double-density disk (360K) in a 5 1/4-inch high-density (1.2M) drive. Follow these steps:

1. Use DOS EDIT to create the following batch file containing the instruction for a special effect changing the color of the screen.

    @ECHO OFF

    ECHO *<Esc>***[37;41m**   *Note:* You must press **Ctrl-P** before pressing the Escape key for EDIT to take the character. Do not type the Esc.

    ECHO THIS FUNCTION FORMATS DOUBLE DENSITY DISKETTES (360K) IN DRIVE A:

    FORMAT A: /F:360

    ECHO *<Esc>***[37;40M**   *Note:* Press **Ctrl-P** before pressing the Escape key for EDIT to take the character.

2. Save the file under the name NEWDISK.BAT.

3. Describe the effects of each line in the batch file NEWDISK.BAT.

4. Execute the batch file NEWDISK. Were the effects what you expected?

Answers to Odd-Numbered Questions

Key Term Matching Questions

1.	k	11.	t
3.	h	13.	a
5.	n	15.	m
7.	l	17.	r
9.	p	19.	i

Multiple-Choice Questions

1. a
3. b
5. e

True/False Questions

1. T
3. F
5. T

Understanding the International Features of DOS

Chapter Summary

Chapter 21 outlines the complicated but sometimes necessary configuration of a PC to various international language standards. Anything you work on that has international implications can cause you inconvenience if you do not adapt your computer to handle various languages and national customs. In this chapter, you learn how to customize your computer system with national language support. The chapter includes the following important points:

- COUNTRY.SYS can provide national formats for currency, the date, and the time.

- KEYB.COM can nationalize your keyboard for certain characters and can be loaded in AUTOEXEC.BAT or CONFIG.SYS, or at the DOS prompt.

- Code page switching can be enabled to use foreign language character sets on your EGA, VGA, or LCD monitor, your keyboard, and a supported printer.

- The COUNTRY.SYS device driver can be placed in CONFIG.SYS with the international country code and an optional code page number.

- To enable code page switching, memory must first be set aside for the language tables by using DISPLAY.SYS and PRINTER.SYS statements in the CONFIG.SYS file. The command to enable national language support, NLSFUNC, then can be entered, specifying the COUNTRY.SYS file.

- To load the code page tables, use the MODE device CODEPAGE PREPARE command—once for your video display and once for your printer.

- Use the new language character set by issuing the CHCP command for the appropriate code page number or by selectively using the MODE device CODEPAGE SELECT command.

Chapter Outline

Active Learning

Key Term Matching

Match the following key terms with the definitions listed after them.

___ 1. KEYB /ID	___ 7. CHCP
___ 2. Ctrl-Alt-F1	___ 8. Ctrl-Alt-F2
___ 3. Code page switching	___ 9. PRINTER.SYS
___ 4. Dead key	___10. DISPLAY.SYS
___ 5. COUNTRY.SYS	___11. NLSFUNC.EXE
___ 6. KEYB /E	___12. EGA.CPI

Definitions

a. This key combination returns you to the keyboard layout installed with KEYB.

b. A configuration file that you can use to display alternate currency, date, and time formats on your system without using other language characters.

c. This file provides support for EGA and VGA displays.

d. This command provides compatible keyboard characters for the selected nationality using one of 20 keyboards specially designed for the supported countries.

e. Putting a statement for this device driver into the CONFIG.SYS file enables code page switching for the video display.

f. Changing to another character table stored in system memory to suit your national language and customs.

g. A command for switching the code page.

h. This keyboard combination switches you to the United States keyboard layout.

i. Putting a statement for this device driver into the CONFIG.SYS file enables code page switching for the printer.

j. The use of this enables you to enter accents with certain vowels and other keys that are used in some languages but not provided on a standard American keyboard.

k. This command provides compatible keyboard characters for the selected nationality using an enhanced keyboard (101- or 102-key style).

l. A command that provides National Language Support for code page switching.

Multiple-Choice Questions

_____ 1. Which of the following files are not associated with internationalizing your computer?

    a. COUNTRY.SYS
    b. KEYB.COM
    c. CODE.EXE
    d. DISPLAY.SYS
    e. PRINTER.SYS

_____ 2. DOS supports _____ national languages or country customs.

    a. 12
    b. 24
    c. 16
    d. 8
    e. 10

_____ 3. Which CONFIG.SYS statement will set up your keyboard for the United Kingdom?

    a. COUNTRY=001,,C:\DOS\COUNTRY.SYS
    b. COUNTRY=999,,C:\DOS\COUNTRY.SYS
    c. COUNTRY=256,,C:\DOS\COUNTRY.SYS
    d. COUNTRY=044,,C:\DOS\COUNTRY.SYS
    e. COUNTRY=444,,C:\DOS\COUNTRY.SYS

_____ 4. The key combination to switch to the United States layout from the country format you have installed is

    a. Ctrl-Alt-F1.
    b. Ctrl-Alt-F2.
    c. Ctrl-Alt-Del.
    d. Ctrl-F1.
    e. Alt-F2.

____ 5. VGA monitors are supported by which of the following screen device code page information files?

     a. LCD.CPI

     b. 5202.CPI

     c. VGA.CPI

     d. 4208.CPI

     e. EGA.CPI

True/False Questions

____ 1. Hercules-type monographic and CGA screens support code page switching with the 4208.CPI screen device code page information file.

____ 2. When you perform a disk directory command (DIR), the date and time stamps for disk files are displayed in whatever national format you have installed.

____ 3. COUNTRY.SYS contains information for video display and keyboards.

____ 4. You can use the KEYB command even if you have not installed any country codes through COUNTRY.SYS.

____ 5. Changing the character set used in your computer to support another language through code page switching does not change the language that DOS uses.

▶ Directed Exercises

Exercise 1: Internationalizing Your Screen Format

In this exercise, you practice changing your screen format to support international formats. This exercise assumes that you are using a computer with a hard disk designated as Drive C: and that CONFIG.SYS is in the root directory of Drive C:. It also assumes that you have a \DOS subdirectory on Drive C: and that a powered-on printer is connected to your computer. Follow these steps:

    1. Make the root directory of Drive C: the default by typing **c:** and pressing **Enter**, and then typing **cd ** and pressing **Enter** again.

2. Copy your existing CONFIG.SYS file to a new file named CONFIG.TXT by typing **copy config.sys config.txt** and pressing **Enter**.

3. Type **dir** at the DOS system prompt and make a hard copy by using **PrintScreen**. Note how the dates and times are displayed.

4. Edit your CONFIG.SYS file with the DOS Editor by typing **edit config.sys** and pressing **Enter**.

5. Enter the following COUNTRY command at the end of your CONFIG.SYS file:

   country=044,,c:\dos\country.sys

6. Save your file to disk and exit the Editor.

7. Reboot your computer by pressing **Ctrl-Alt-Del** to activate the country change.

8. Return to the root directory of Drive C: by following the instructions in step 1, if necessary.

9. Again, type **dir** at the DOS system prompt and make a hard copy by using **PrintScreen**.

   a. Make a particular note how the dates and times are displayed.

   b. Compare the dates and times to what was produced in step 3.

   c. Are they the same or different? Why?

10. If you are not immediately continuing to exercise 2, delete the changed CONFIG.SYS file and then type the following:

   ren config.txt config.sys.

Exercise 2: Internationalizing Your Keyboard

This exercise is designed to give you practice changing your screen format to support international formats and is intended to immediately follow exercise 1. This exercise assumes that you are using a computer with a hard disk designated as Drive C: and that CONFIG.SYS is in the root directory of Drive C:. It also assumes that you have a \DOS subdirectory on Drive C: and that a powered-on printer is connected to your computer. Follow these steps:

1. If you are not doing this exercise immediately after doing exercise 1, be sure to complete exercise 1 before continuing.

2. At the DOS prompt, type **keyb** and press **Enter**. Copy down the message that appears on-screen or print a hard copy for further reference.

3. Type **keyb uk,,c:\dos\keyboard.sys** and press **Enter**.

4. Type **keyb** again and compare the message to the message received in step 2.

5. Press the following keys and write down what the screen's response is to each one:

   a. #

   b. \

   c. @

   d. "

   e. |

6. Press **Ctrl-Alt-F1** to return to the United States keyboard layout.

7. Press the following keys a second time and compare the screen's response to what you received in step 5:

   a. #

   b. \

   c. @

   d. "

   e. |

Answers to Odd-Numbered Questions

Key Term Matching Questions

1. d		7. g	
3. f		9. i	
5. b		11. l	

Multiple-Choice Questions

1. c

3. d

5. e

True/False Questions

1. F

3. F

5. T

Notes

Notes

Notes

Notes